THE FUNNIEST JOKE BOOK IN AMERICA

VOLUME 1

"How to Tell & to Memorize Jokes"
"When & Where to Tell Them"

DOC MARTIN

THE FUNNIEST JOKE BOOK IN AMERICA
Volume 1
Copyright © 2021 by Doc Martin

Library of Congress Control Number: 2021911881
ISBN-13:   Paperback: 978-1-64749-502-2
            ePub: 978-1-64749-503-9

Printed in the United States of America

 GoTo Publish

GoToPublish LLC
1-888-337-1724
www.gotopublish.com
info@gotopublish.com

CONTENTS

And Other Assorted Jokes Throughout

THE FUNNIEST JOKE BOOK IN AMERICA

Prepared by Duane Martin

Forward

One of the greatest assets that I feel anyone could have is a positive attitude. There are things that you can do nothing about but you do have the option to be optimistic to be positive and be outgoing in expressing a good, healthy, and positive attitude. Your self-image is directly impacted by the attitude you chose to maintain, and the friends that you wish to spend your time with reflect that. The consequences of poor attitudes not only deteriorate one's self image and consequential ability to respond to others in a productive manner but can also affect one's physical health.

The ability to express one's self to others comes in various forms. Body language is one way of communication, the way one dresses, the way they act and the way that they speak are still others that create positive opinions or negative ones. The statement is made, "The way you act is so loud, I can't hear what you are saying!" Is so true.

It is my opinion that if I did not have sense of humor I would not have any sense at all. What I mean by that is that humor can lift your spirit when you are in one of the darkest times in your life if you chose to let it. The scripture puts it this way, "A merry heart doeth good like a medicine. . . ." Prov. 17:22. I have personally been through some major changes in my life that could have taken a negative toll on me personally had I allowed it.

People ask where I grew up, well first of all, I never grew up, but I was raised in a small house in a small hometown, on a hill just above the railroad track, named Veedersburg, Indiana. My father committed suicide when he was 32 and I was 11. My mother remarried and divorced and I followed the same path of having been married and divorced twice. I have a great deal that I can feel negatively about but I have chosen to accept the good with the bad and humor is one of my closest friends.

In my younger years, after my father had died, I had a difficult time learning how to meet people and developing friendships. Telling jokes became my forte and I could make people laugh and feel comfortable around me. After a while I realized that it was a mask, that I was so terribly concerned of other's response and felt accepted if they laughed and inadequate if they did not. I left that mask in my past but there is a tendency every now and then to reach back and put it on.

I try to stay away from joke telling if I am ill at ease with my surroundings and only tell them when I do feel comfortable with whomever I am with.

HOW TO TELL A JOKE

This section might seem a bit elementary to some but I strongly recommend that you read it for being successful as a good joke teller or comedian, as it will be important to you. I remember the very first off colored joke I heard. I was around 11 years of age then and remember the individual, Mr. Wood, who told me that joke in my hometown, Veedersburg, Indiana. He was and is presently a carpenter and on that day he was working on pastor Jim Dyson's parsonage. I was walking home from school and stopped to chat since he was my next-door neighbor. The way that he told the joke was so humorous and he said it just with the right inflection that I could not stop laughing. I remember laughing so hard all the way down to the intersection. Half way across the street I finally got the joke and laughed all the harder. I wanted to share it with my mom at the table a few minutes later but was fearful that she would wash my mouth out with soap.

The important point that I realized then is that the primary effect of a joke is simply the way in which one tells it, in other words, the delivery. Some people don't understand this and their jokes lose much of its flavor. Every time I hear a good joke I repeat it over and over again, studying my pauses, my inflections, facial expressions, tone of voice, accent I chose to use, etc. until I feel it is refined enough and I am very comfortable with it. Then I will tell it to 5 or 6 different people and watch their response. In this way I not only test the effectiveness of the joke but I come to memorize it quite well. A subject I will discuss later.

It is also important to be in good taste and to know your audience. Sell your audience! Any professional speaker will tell you that the first few minutes, probably less than two, is the critical period of time in determining if you will win your audience or lose them. It becomes even more critical and you have less time when you are joke telling. So be sure to use some of your proven favorites up front, make the first two or three a grand slam and they will listen because you sold your audience on your ability. If people are not responding it may be that the mood setting, or ambiance of that particular group is not conducive to joke telling. This does not mean that you can't tell a joke in just about any setting. I have told a joke or two at a funeral because those whom I was with needed to lighten up a bit and it was acceptable. However, you need to be keenly aware in delicate situations such as this, not to offend someone and to know when he or she are not ready for lightheartedness.

In many settings, such as a bar, where there is a great deal of noise and distraction, it is good to keep jokes very brief. You can tell short jokes that are to the point. Get in and get out quickly. If you tell longer ones, cut corners and get to the point or you will lose your audience. I have seen many who fail on this point. They presume people will stay with them and so they elongate their jokes. Before they get to their punch line the audience has lost interest.

Too much of any good thing can be bad and you can learn how to read an audience. To know when it is acceptable to continue and, most importantly, know when to stop and not overdo it. It is far better to stop a little premature than to continue and lose your audience as it can start to be annoying to them. I did this with my uncle Jerry and I should have stopped sooner.

This is my third book and my second completed work, the first is a book of poetry, "In Sunshine & Rain." and you can purchase it online. Poetry is a beautiful way of expression but fewer audiences that respond. A joke you can tell to almost anyone with a culture, as it is, in the United States. Europe is more conducive to poetry. I have only met one person in my life that claimed that jokes were not funny to her that she simply did not get the humor. That is sad because we all need to laugh, even at ourselves at times. Life is too short and should never be taken too seriously. The Bible teaches us that, "Laughter maketh good like a medicine." but also teaches against foolish jesting.

HOW TO MEMORIZE JOKE'S

AND THE CORRESPONDING BENEFITS

Memorizing was not always an easy task for me in my youth but I have learned methodologies that assisted me in my memory capabilities. I tend to memorize quite easily now and wish to share some of techniques that have helped me with you. There are many who say that they cannot remember jokes. This is simply because they do not file them in their memory in a way they can readily access them. When you tell them a joke or two that triggers their memory, they will inevitably come back with, "Oh, I remember that one!" It only took the proper prodding to help them reach back in their mental filing cabinet to retrieve it. This is because their files are not well organized.

I subconsciously see a setting in every joke I hear. I see a situation, a physical dwelling, a city or whatever comes to mind and envision it when I tell a joke. Believe me it will help you every time. Many times I will ask someone, "Give me a subject to tell a joke on," and in almost every instance I can recall one. This is because I see word pictures.

If I asked you to tell me a joke about doctors, lawyers, builders, farmers, preachers, bartenders, the elderly, or whatever, I am sure you can think of a few in at least one or two of these categories. This is because I prompted you just as others prompt you by telling you a joke. This is categorical methodology, but it works. How about Engineer, Redneck, Texan, or Martian jokes, these are all categorical?

Situational Jokes would be more like a truck or bus driver or the letter carrier was driving along or was walking down the road, and jokes regarding Little Johnny, Helen Keller, Presidents, or politicians. These jokes have their own category, which I would define as Object Jokes. These would include every day personal and impersonal items such as the telephone, washing machine, automobile, persons, dogs, cats, ducks, ships, and airplanes.

How about Sport Jokes: Golfing, football, basketball, skiing, and hockey. These are all in categories and the various titles that you file jokes under in your memory will assist in prompting you of a setting to where you see the joke. A picture is worth a thousand words and I am referring to pictures that you see in your mind. If you begin telling jokes in a category, such as old age, divorce, or whatever, you can continue in that category by using a method I call "Linking."

When you link jokes in certain categories it makes it easier for you to remember by association and more easily segued. By this I mean, moving smoothly from one joke to another in a much more natural fashion. This will help open the door for you and you will not need to say, as many others, "I just cannot remember jokes!"

One of the best joke tellers I have ever met is Greg Abrahams. He tells many Cajun jokes. Many of the jokes, which I had already known, Greg would put a Cajun accent to it and make it come out unique and hilarious. What he is doing is telling a story by which you can see and laugh at our human character.

The first time I met Greg it was at a Super bowl party. As he told the jokes I thought to myself, "Oh perfect, I will tell this one next." I was astonished when he ended that he segued or segued to the same joke I was thinking. I thought to myself, I will tell this one next and Greg took it again. This is because he has learned the art of linking sequential jokes and Transition from one to another by association. This assists in creating an even flow. One joke reminds you of another and still another until you have an entire portfolio of jokes in any given category. When you deplete that category just change to another category and off you go.

Many of the jokes in this book are under categories and will assist you in memorizing and filing it in your mind if you give it a little time. I have been told that I have a fantastic memory but there was one time in my life that I did not feel that way or could not recite as well as I do today. I am going to share with you my Dynamic Memory Technique (DMT).

You can use it to memorize anything. It is a very simple method and anyone can do it if they apply themselves. I learned it while in college and memorizing material word for word. I have virtually tens of thousands of sequential words in memory. Your brain has a tremendous ability to memorize. The brain is like a muscle and if you will use it you will find it strengthening and will be surprised of what it can produce. I do not care how old a person gets, they can be as sharp mentally as they wish to apply themselves.

This is not a book about memory but you can benefit by increasing your memory in many other ways than joke telling. Pick up a good book on memory sometime and it will give you methods to memorize. Now for my method of memory I developed and it works for me. I call it (DMT) Dynamic Memory Technique: I will ask you to try it for the next seven days:

In the evening, before you retire for the night, read a few of your favorite jokes. Begin with shorter ones and then work up to longer ones. You may work on one or more but only work on one at a time. Read it at least three times. Then try to recite it from memory. It will also greatly assist you if you write it out. Do not worry about what you forget, go back and write what you didn't remember down. Now try to quote it again. Then try to recite it again. Use this method before going to bed but be sure to be able to quote the entire joke seven times before doing so. When you wake up in the morning you will be surprised how well you remember the joke. Try it now!

The more you practice this method the easier it will get. Again this is not just a memory that is applicable to joke telling. You can use it for anything such as Memorizing Bible chapters, preparing for a job interview, preparing for a speech, poetry, and on and on. I can quote 90% of my book of poetry by memory.

When you do memorize you will find that your words flow much easier. I call this, "Better said than read." You are not choppy but smooth. You are more comfortable to know when to pause, when to raise your voice a little higher or lower, when to quicken your speech or use an inflection or dialect. You can then become very creative.

Change the joke to a cleft pallet, a stutterer, a foreign accent maybe Italian, Mexican, or even Cajun. Use whatever works for you. In this way you will be comfortable not mimicking someone else's style but being yourself. This is what makes comedians so unique from each other. It's their style that makes them personable and appreciated.

IN DEDICATION

With the content being so versatile there are some who may be offended. It is very difficult to dedicate this book to any specific person so I will simply dedicate it to its audience. Those who have learned as I have, that without a sense of humor it is very probable that you wouldn't have any sense at all.

If the content is offensive to anyone it was not my desire or intention to do so. Treat this book like a piece of chicken and if there are parts, such as the bones, which are not of your liking, just throw it out and enjoy what you do like. This book therefore is dedicated to you, the reader.

Duane Martin

ANTHOLOGY

Through the years I have come across several jokes, limericks, and quotations from many different people. Quotes, short stories, miracles and angels is a very large book that I have not entitled nor published yet. I learned much humor which was shared by friends, relatives, or acquaintances. I have held many in memory for years. I have found them to be enjoyable and therefore have taken the time to include them in this book.

Basically jokes are considered to be public domain. It is impossible however to know for sure if any herein have been authored and published without actually locating it in a work where the author's name is given. This becomes increasingly difficult with photocopies of photocopies where there is no authorship identified, or jokes found online. Should there be anyone whose work appears here without proper arrangement or proper acknowledgment, please allow me to do so in the next printing. It is not my desire or intention to use anyone's material without permission or proper credit.

I have also made diligent effort to trace the authorship of the jokes that I have in this book and have not included any that I know to be authored and copyrighted by another. All whom I have located as authors I have given proper acknowledgment.

Attorney Jokes:

WHO'S WORSE? INSURANCE COMPANIES OR LAWYERS...

Unfortunately this story is an urban legend but it is still funny. It came across an internet email and supposedly was the 1st place winner in the recent Criminal Lawyers Award Contest.

A Charlotte, NC, lawyer purchased a box of very rare and expensive cigars then insured them against fire, among other things. Within a month, having smoked his entire stockpile of these great cigars, and without yet having made even his first premium payment on the policy, the lawyer filed a claim against the insurance company. In his claim, the lawyer stated the cigars were lost "in a series of small fires."

The insurance company refused to pay, citing the obvious reason: that the man had consumed the cigars in the normal fashion. The lawyer sued... and won!

In delivering the ruling the judge agreed with the insurance company that the claim was frivolous. The Judge stated nevertheless, that the lawyer held a policy from the company in which it had warranted that the cigars were insurable and also guaranteed that it would insure them against fire, without defining what is considered to be "unacceptable fire" and was obligated to pay the claim.

Rather than endure a lengthy and costly appeal process, the insurance company accepted the ruling and paid 15,000.00 to the lawyer for his loss of the rare cigars lost in the "fires."

NOW FOR THE BEST PART...

After the lawyer cashed the check, the insurance company had him arrested on 24 counts of ARSON! With his own insurance claim, and testimony from the previous case being used against him, the lawyer was convicted of intentionally burning his insured property and sentenced him to 24 months in jail and a $24,000.00 fine.

What is the difference between a prostitute and an attorney?

1. A prostitute will stop screwing you after you are dead.

2. With an attorney you pay for the screwing you got and with a hooker you pay for the screwing you get.

Why are sperm and attorneys alike?

One in a million, turn out to be human.

What is the difference between an attorney and a Rooster?

A rooster clucks defiant!

Why do they bury attorneys 12 feet under?

Because they say that attorneys are really good people deep down.

A lawyer, a doctor, and a priest were on a boat that capsized in shark-infested waters. They ate the doctor and the priest. Why didn't they eat the lawyer? Professional Courtesy!

What is the difference between an attorney and a Carp? One is a whale-bellied, slime-eating, scum-sucking, scavenging parasite and the other, of course, is a fish.

One day God calls Satan up on the telephone and says with a sneer, "So, how's it going down there in hell?" Satan replies, "Hey, things are going great. We've got air conditioning and flush toilets and escalators, and there's no telling what this engineer is going to come up with next." God replies, "What??? You've got an engineer? That's a mistake! He should never have gotten down there; send him up here." Satan says, "No way.

I like having an engineer on the staff, and I'm keeping him." God says, "Send him back up here or I'll sue." Satan laughs uproariously and answers, "Yeah, right. And just where are YOU going to get a lawyer?"

A true story that happened to me about something I should have said but was a little shy to say it. It is one of those wish I did, could have done, or should have done.

You see, I went to an attorney over a matter, and he changed the subject and in saying just how good he was as an attorney, he got a man off after stabbing his wife 27 times. What I thought to say but didn't was, "I would have left him after the first time!"

A blind bunny and blind snake were passing each other in the woods. They began talking to each other and the blind bunny asked the snake if he could wrap himself around him and to tell him what he was since he was blind from birth and didn't know. So the snake wrapped himself around the bunny and told him, "Well, you are furry, have a small tail, and have pointy ears. You are a bunny!" The snake then asked the bunny to do the same, so the bunny starting feeling the snake and said, "You are cold, slimy, you have a forked tongue and no balls. You must be an attorney!"

It was a sexual harassment case, and it had been a long day. The young lady accusing her boss said that she was too embarrassed to repeat the words that he said to her. The Judge suggested she write them down and that the words be shown to himself and the jury.

She passed the note, which read - 'Go and take your knickers off, then come sit on my knee and have a drink with me tonight', to the Judge, who then passed it on to Fred, the foreperson of the jury.

Fred went to pass it on to the next juror, a middle-aged lady, who had nodded off in the stuffy courtroom. He had to nudge her to bring her back to full consciousness.

She woke, read the note, smiled, read it a second time, winked, and nodded at Fred, then put the note in her handbag.

What is the difference between a lawyer lying in the road and a skunk lying in the road? There are skid marks in front of the skunk.

How do you know when it is cold outside?

Answer: When an attorney has his hands in his own pockets.

Scientists are now using attorneys for testing instead of rats for three basic reasons:

1. There are more attorneys than rats

2. Attorneys do things that rats won't

3. The scientists don't get as attached to attorneys as they do with rats.

A lady who was getting ready to get married visited a bridal shop and found a beautiful white dress that she liked. She informed the sales lady that she was getting married for her fourth time and wanted the white dress. The sales lady politely suggested that she select something more off white since the white dress was usually the first wedding dress, a symbol of virginity.

She then told the sales lady that she didn't understand. She went on to say, "My first husband was a psychiatrist and all that he wanted to do was just talk about it. My second husband was a gynecologist and all that he wanted to do was look at it. My third husband was a stamp collector and man am I gonna' miss him." 'So what is your fourth husband?' the sales lady inquired. "Oh, he's an attorney, now I know I'm gonna' get screwed!"

For 3 years, the young attorney had been taking his brief vacations at this country inn. The last time there, he'd finally managed to have an affair with the innkeeper's daughter. Looking forward to an exciting few days, he dragged his suitcase up the stairs of the inn, and then he stopped short. There sat his lover with an infant on her lap! "Helen, why didn't you write when you learned you were pregnant, he replied?" "I would have rushed up here, we could have gotten married, and the baby would have my name!" "Well," she said, "when my folks found out about my condition, we sat up all night just a talkin' and talkin.' We decided it would be better to have a bastard in the family than a lawyer."

On their way to a justice of the peace to get married, a couple had a fatal car accident. The couple found themselves sitting outside Heaven's Gate waiting on St. Peter to do an intake. While waiting, they wondered if they could possibly get married in Heaven. St. Peter finally showed up and they asked him. St. Peter said, "I don't know, this is the first time anyone has asked." "Let me go find out." and he left.

The couple sat and waited for an answer for three months... and they began to wonder if they really should get married in Heaven, with the eternal aspect of it all. "What if it doesn't work out?" they wondered, "Are we stuck together forever?"

St. Peter returned after yet another month, looking somewhat bedraggled. "Yes," he informed the couple, "you can get married in Heaven." "Great," said the couple, "but what if things don't work out? Could we also get a divorce in Heaven?" St. Peter, red-faced, slammed his clipboard onto the ground. "What's wrong?", asked the frightened couple. "COME ON!" St. Peter shouted, "It took me three months to find a priest up here! Do you have any idea how long it will take me to find an Attorney?"

A blonde and a lawyer are seated next to each other on a flight from LA to NY. The lawyer asks if she would like to play a fun game. The blonde, tired, just wants to take a nap, politely declines and rolls over to the window to catch a few winks.

The lawyer persists and explains that the game is easy and a lot of fun. He explains, "I ask you a question, and if you don't know the answer, you pay me $5.00, and Visa-Versa." Again, she declines and tries to get some sleep.

The lawyer, now agitated, says, "Okay, if you don't know the answer you pay me $5.00, and if I don't know the answer, I will pay you $500.00." This catches the blonde's attention and, figuring there will be no end to this torment unless she plays, agrees to the game. The lawyer asks the first question. "What's the distance from the Earth to the moon?"

The blonde doesn't say a word, reaches into her purse, pulls out a $5.00 bill and hands it to the lawyer. Okay says the lawyer, your turn. She asks the lawyer, "What goes up a hill with three legs and comes down with four legs?"

The lawyer, puzzled, takes out his laptop computer and searches all his references, no answer. He taps into the air phone with his modem and searches the net and the library of congress, no answer. Frustrated, he sends Emails to all his friends and coworkers, to no avail. After hunting for an hour, he wakes the blonde, and hands her $500.00.

The blonde says, "Thank you," and turns back to get some more sleep. The lawyer, who is more than a little miffed, wakes the blonde and asks, "Well, what's the answer?"

Without a word, the blonde reaches into her purse, hands the lawyer $5.00, and goes back to sleep.

And you thought blondes were dumb...

A man and his dog were walking along a road. The man was enjoying the scenery, when it suddenly occurred to him that he was dead. He remembered dying, and that the dog had been dead for years. He wondered where the road was leading them.

After a while, they came to a high, white stone wall along one side of the road. It looked like fine marble. At the top of a long hill, it was broken by a tall arch that glowed in the sunlight. When he was standing before it, he saw a magnificent gate in the arch that looked like mother of pearl, and the street that led to the gate looked like pure gold.

He and the dog walked toward the gate, and as he got closer, he saw a man at a desk to one side. When he was close enough, he called out, "Excuse me, where are we?" "This is Heaven, sir," the man answered. "Wow! Would you happen to have some water?" the man asked. "Of course, sir. Come right in, and I'll have some ice water brought right up." The man gestured, and the gate began to open. "Can my friend," gesturing toward his dog, "come in, too?" the traveler asked. "I'm sorry, sir, but we don't accept pets."

The man thought a moment and then turned back toward the road and continued the way he had been going. After another long walk, and at the top of another long hill, he came to a dirt road, which led through a farm gate that looked as if it had never been closed. There was no fence. As he approached the gate, he saw a man inside, leaning against a tree and reading a book. "Excuse me!" he called to the reader. "Do you have any water?" "Yeah, sure, there's a pump over there" The man pointed to a place that couldn't be seen from outside the gate. "Come on in." "How about my friend here?" the traveler gestured to the dog. "There should be a bowl by the pump."

They went through the gate, and sure enough, there was an old-fashioned hand pump with a bowl beside it. The traveler filled the bowl and took a long drink himself, then he gave some to the dog. When they were full, he and the dog walked back toward the man who was standing by the tree waiting for them.

"What do you call this place?" the traveler asked. "This is Heaven," was the answer. "Well, that's confusing," the traveler said. "The man down the road said that was Heaven, too." "Oh, you mean the place with the gold street and pearly gates? Nope. That's Hell." "Doesn't it make you mad for them to use your name like that?" "No. I can see how you might think so, but we're just happy that they screen out the folks who'll leave their best friends behind."

After starting her own business, an investment counselor found that her business was going so well that she needed to get in-house counsel. So she began interviewing young lawyers. "In this business," she stated to one of her first applicants, "Our personal integrity must be beyond question. Do you consider yourself an honest lawyer, Mr. Ford?" "I certainly do!" replied the lawyer. "I'm so honest that after my father loaned me fifteen thousand dollars for my education, I paid back every penny after my very first case." The investment counselor was impressed. "What sort of case was it?" she asked. The lawyer pressed his lips tightly for a moment before finally answering, "He sued me for the money."

I worked for a while at a Wal-Mart store, selling sporting goods. As an employee of Wal-Mart you are sometimes required to make store-wide pages, e.g., "I have a customer in hardware that needs assistance at the paint counter." One night a tentative female voice came over the intercom system with the following message: "I have a customer by the balls in toys that needs assistance."

Jack, Larry, and Gary went to the rodeo. Unfortunately, a big bull jumped the fence into the stands and they were trampled. Being good God-fearing men, they ascended to Heaven where they were met at the gate by St. Peter. He said, "Welcome to Heaven gentlemen. I must warn you that we do have rules here in Heaven. If you break the rules, you will be punished. One rule is, don't step on a duck. If you step on a duck, the duck quacks, then they all quack and it just goes on and on."

That sounded simple enough. They passed through the Pearly Gates and there were ducks everywhere! Soon, Jack was hurrying along, and he stepped on a duck. When the duck quacked, they all quacked, and it was a terrible racket, and it just went on and on. Pretty soon here came St. Peter and he had a very homely woman in tow. "I warned you that if you broke the rules, you would be punished." He chained the homely little woman to Jack with a short piece of chain and said, "You will be together forever," and walked away.

Sometime later Larry stepped on a duck. The duck quacked, then they all quacked and there was a terrible commotion that went on and on. Here came St. Peter with an even homelier woman. "I warned you that if you broke the rules that you would be punished." He chained the woman to Larry with a short chain and said, "You will be together thru eternity," and walked away.

Well, Gary was very careful not to step on a duck & one day St. Peter came up to him with a gorgeous blonde. Then he them all together and said, "You will be together forever" and walked away. Gary said, "Wow, what did I do to deserve this? "Well, I don't know what you did," said the blonde, "but I stepped on a duck.

{This is one I tell very well as I can do a great Donald Duck and have been on two radio stations and was a Disk Jockey in my younger years.}

Donald and Daisy Duck go to a hotel room where they planned to spend the night together. When Donald started to get a little frisky and things were warming up, Donald pauses, puts his clothes on and goes down to the front desk. The little store was just beside the front desk so Donald went in and asked if they had any prophylactics. The clerk said that they did, and would Donald wish to have it put on his bill, to which Donald replied, "Hell no, I would suffocate!"

One day, a teacher, a garbage collector and a lawyer wound up together at the Pearly Gates. St. Peter informed them that in order to get into Heaven, they would each have to answer one question. St. Peter addressed the teacher and asked, "What was the name of the ship that crashed into an iceberg? They just made a movie about it."

The teacher answered quickly, "That would be the Titanic." St. Peter let him through the gate. St. Peter turned to the garbage man and decided to make the question a little harder, "How many people died on the ship?" Fortunately for him, the trash man had just seen the movie and answered, "About 1,500." "That's right! You may enter." St. Peter then turned to the lawyer. "Name them."

A New York divorce lawyer died and arrived at the pearly gates. Saint Peter asked him, "What have you done to merit entrance into Heaven?" The lawyer thought a moment, then said, "A week ago, I gave a quarter to a homeless person on the street."

Saint Peter asked Gabriel to check this out in the record, and after a moment Gabriel affirmed that this was true. Saint Peter said, "Well, that's fine, but it's not really quite enough to get you into Heaven." The lawyer said, "Wait! There's more! Three years ago I also gave a homeless person a quarter." Saint Peter nodded to Gabriel, who after a moment nodded back, affirming thus it had been verified.

Saint Peter then whispered to Gabriel, "Well, what do you suggest we do with this fellow?" Gabriel gave the lawyer a sidelong glance and then said to Saint Peter, "Let's give him back his 50 cents and tell him to go to Hell."

Dilbert: What should we call a habitat for worthless and disgusting little creatures? Dogbert: Law school.

One day a Jew, a Hindu, and a lawyer all arrived at their hotel to find that there had been a mix-up with the bookings, and that there was only one room left for them to share. The manager explained that this room only had two beds, but that there was a barn at a neighboring farm which the farmer, an old friend of his, would let one of them sleep in free of charge. They complained a bit, but since there was nowhere else to go, the Jew graciously said he'd sleep in the barn.

The Hindu and the lawyer were just settling down to sleep in their room, when there was a knock on the door. It was the Jew. "I'm sorry," he said, "but there's a pig in that barn and because I'm Jewish I feel uncomfortable about sharing the barn with it." "No problem," said the Hindu. "I'll sleep out there instead." So off he went to the barn, leaving the lawyer and the Jew to share the room.

They were just settling down to sleep, when there was a knock on the door. It was the Hindu. "I'm sorry," he said, "but there's a cow in that barn and because I'm a Hindu I feel uncomfortable about sharing the barn with it." The lawyer grudgingly agreed to give up his bed and stomped off to the barn, leaving the Jew and the Hindu to share the room. The Jew and the Hindu were just settling down to sleep, when there was a knock on the door. It was the cow and the pig.

A lawyer opened the door of his BMW, when suddenly a car came along and hit his door, ripping it off completely. When the police arrived at the scene, the lawyer was hopping up and down with rage, complaining bitterly about the damage to his precious BMW. "Officer, look what they've done to my Beeeemer!!!" he shrieked.

"You lawyers are so materialistic, you make me sick!!!" retorted the officer, "You're so worried about your stupid BMW, that you didn't even notice that your left arm was ripped off!!!"

"Oh no...." replied the lawyer, looking down and noticing for the first time the bloody stump where his left arm had once been. "Where's my Rolex???"

A lawyer named Strange died, and his friend asked the tombstone maker to inscribe on his tombstone, "Here lays Strange, an honest man, and a lawyer." The inscriber insisted that such an inscription would be confusing, for passers-by would tend to think that three men were buried under the stone. However he suggested an alternative. He would inscribe, "Here lays a man who was both honest and a lawyer." "That way, whenever anyone walked by the tombstone and read it, they would be certain to remark, 'That's Strange!"

One day God calls Satan up on the telephone and says with a sneer, "So, how's it going down there in hell?" Satan replies, "Hey, things are going great. We've got air conditioning and flush toilets and escalators, and there's no telling what this engineer is going to come up with next." God replies, "What??? You've got an engineer? That's a mistake! He should never have gotten down there; send him up here." Satan says, "No way. I like having an engineer on the staff, and I'm keeping him." God says, "Send him back up here or I'll sue." Satan laughs uproariously and answers, "Yeah, right. And just where are YOU going to get a lawyer?"

A BILL TO REGULATE THE HUNTINGAND HARVESTING OF ATTORNEYS

US Government Department of Fish and "Wildlife" Sec. 1432

1432-01. Any person with a valid state rodent or armadillo hunting license may also hunt and harvest attorneys for recreational and sporting (Non-commercial) purposes.

1432-02. Taking of attorneys with traps or deadfalls is permitted. The use of currency as bait is prohibited.

1432-04. It is unlawful to chase, herd, or harvest attorneys from a snow machine, helicopter, or aircraft.

1432-05. It shall be unlawful to shout "Whiplash", "Ambulance", or "Free Scotch" for the purpose of trapping attorneys.

1432-06. It shall be unlawful to hunt attorneys within 100 yards of BMW, Mercedes, or Porsche dealerships, except on Wednesday afternoons.

1432-07. It shall be unlawful to hunt attorneys within 200 yards of courtrooms, law libraries, health spas, ambulances, or hospitals.

1432-08. If an attorney is elected to government office, it is not necessary to have a license to hunt, trap, or possess the same.

1432-09. It shall be illegal for a hunter to disguise himself as a reporter, drug dealer, female legal clerk, accident victim, physician, chiropractor, bookie, or tax accountant for the purpose of hunting attorneys.

1432-10 The willful killing of attorneys with a motor vehicle is prohibited, unless such vehicle is an ambulance being driven in reverse. If an attorney is accidentally struck by a motor vehicle, the dead attorney should be removed to the roadside, and the vehicle should proceed to the nearest car wash.

1432-11. Bag Limits Per Day: Yellow-bellied Sidewinders:

2 Two-faced Tort-feasors:

1 Back-stabbing Divorce Litigators:

3 Horn-rimmed Cut-throats:

2 Minutiae-advocating Chickens:

4 Honest Attorneys: 0 (Protected, Endangered species.)

A lawyer dies in a car accident on his 40th birthday and finds himself greeted at the Pearly Gates by a brass band. Saint Peter runs over, shakes his hand and says "Congratulations!!!"

"Congratulations for what?" asks the lawyer. "Congratulations for what?!?!?" says Saint Peter. "We're celebrating the fact that you lived to be 160 years old." "But that's not true," says the lawyer. "I only lived to be forty." "That's impossible," says Saint Peter. "We've added up all your time sheets."

Two lawyers are stranded on a deserted island, nothing around them for miles and miles but water. They've been stranded here for quite some time, so they've gotten quite bored with one another.

One of the lawyers tells the other he's going to climb to the top of the tree (the only thing on the island) to see if he can possibly see a rescue team coming. The other lawyer tells him he's crazy and that he's just wasting his time and won't see anything. But the lawyer proceeds to climb to the top of the tree anyway. He's up there only a short time when the lawyer down on the ground hears him say, "Wow! I can't believe my eyes! I don't believe this is true!"

So the lawyer on the ground says, "What do you see? I think you're hallucinating and you should come down right now," So the lawyer reluctantly climbs down the tree and proceeds to tell his friend that he saw a naked blonde woman floating face up headed toward their island.

The other lawyer starts to laugh, thinking his friend has surely lost his mind. But within a few minutes, up floats a naked blonde woman, face up, totally unconscious. The two lawyers go over to where she is, and one says to the other, "Well, you know it's been a long time... do you think we should screw her?" The other lawyer responds, "Out of what?"

In a long line of people waiting for a bank teller, one guy suddenly started massaging the back of the person in front of him.

Surprised, the man in front turned and snarled, "Just what the hell are you doing?" "Well," said the guy, "You see, I'm a chiropractor and I could see that you were tense, so I had to massage your back. Sometimes I just can't help practicing my art!" "That's the stupidest thing I've ever heard!" the guy replied. "I'm a lawyer. Do you see me screwing the guy in front of me?"

Did you hear about the new sushi bar that caters exclusively to lawyers? It's called Sosumi.

How are an apple and a lawyer alike? They both look good hanging from a tree.

How can a pregnant woman tell that she's carrying a future lawyer? She has an uncontrollable craving for baloney.

What do you throw to a drowning lawyer? His partners!

A small-town prosecuting attorney called his first witness to the stand in a trial-a grandmotherly, elderly woman. He approached her and asked, "Mrs. Jones, do you know me?" She responded, "Why, yes, I do know you Mr. Williams. I've known you since you were a young boy. And frankly, you've been a big disappointment to me. You lie, you cheat on your wife, and you manipulate people and talk about them behind their backs. You think you're a rising big shot when you haven't the brains to realize you never will amount to anything more than a two-bit paper pusher. Yes, I know you."

The lawyer was stunned. Not knowing what else to do he pointed across the room and asked, "Mrs. Jones, do you know the defense attorney?" She again replied, "Why, yes I do. I've known Mr. Bradley since he was a youngster, too. I used to baby-sit him for his parents. And he, too, has been a real disappointment to me. He's lazy, bigoted, and he has a drinking problem. The man can't build a normal relationship with anyone and his law practice is one of the shoddiest in the entire state. Yes, I know him."

At this point, the judge rapped the courtroom to silence and called both counselors to the bench. In a very quiet voice, he said with menace, "If either of you asks her if she knows me, you'll be in jail for contempt."

If a lawyer and an IRS agent were both drowning, and you could only save one of them, would you go to lunch or read the paper?

What do you call 25 attorneys buried up to their chins in cement? Not enough cement.

What do you call 25 skydiving lawyers?   Skeet!

What does a lawyer do after sex?   Pays the bill!

What does a lawyer get when you give him Viagra? - Taller.

What happens when you cross a pig with a lawyer? Nothing. There are some things a pig won't do.

What's the difference between a lawyer and a vulture? Removable wingtips!

Why did God make snakes before lawyers? - To practice.

You're trapped in a room with a tiger, a rattlesnake and a lawyer. You have a gun with two bullets. What should you do...? Shoot the lawyer, slight pause, - Twice!

An elderly spinster called the lawyer's office and told the receptionist she wanted to see the lawyer about having a will prepared. The receptionist suggested they set up an appointment for a convenient time for the spinster to come into the office. The woman replied, "You must understand, I've lived alone all my life, I rarely see anyone, and I don't like to go out. Would it be possible for the lawyer to come to my house?" The receptionist checked with the attorney who agreed and he went to the spinster's home for the meeting to discuss her estate and the will.

The lawyer's first question was, "Would you please tell me what you have in assets and how you'd like them to be distributed under your will?" She replied, "Besides the furniture and accessories you see here, I have $40,000 in my savings account at the bank." "Tell me," the lawyer asked, "how would you like the $40,000 to be distributed?" The spinster said, "Well, as I've told you, I've lived a reclusive life, people have hardly ever noticed me, so I'd like them to notice when I pass on. I'd like to provide $35,000 for my funeral." The lawyer remarked, "Well, for $35,000 you will be able to have a funeral that will certainly be noticed and will leave a lasting impression on anyone who may not have taken much note of you! But tell me," He continued, what would you like to do with the remaining $5,000?"

The spinster replied, "As you know, I've never married, I've lived alone almost my entire life, and in fact I've never slept with a man. I'd like you to use the $5,000 to arrange for a man to sleep with me." "This is a very unusual request," the lawyer said, adding, "but I'll see what I can do to arrange it and get back to you."

That evening, the lawyer was at home telling his wife about the eccentric spinster and her weird request. After thinking about how much she could do around the house with $5,000, and with a bit of coaxing, she got her husband to agree to provide the service himself. She said, "I'll drive you over tomorrow morning, and wait in the car until you're finished."

The next morning, she drove him to the spinster's house and waited while he went into the house. She waited for over an hour, but her husband didn't come out. So she blew the car horn. Shortly, the upstairs bedroom window opened, the lawyer stuck his head out and yelled, "Pick me up tomorrow, she's going to let the County bury her!"

These are things people actually said in court, word for word:

Q: What is your date of birth?

A: July fifteenth.

Q: What year?

A: Every year.

Q: What gear were you in the moment of impact?

A: Gucci sweets and Reeboks.

Q: And in what ways does it affect your memory?

A: I forget.

Q: You forget. Can you give us an example of something that you have forgotten?

Q: How old is your son, the one living with you?

A: 38 or 35, I can't remember which.

Q: How long has he lived with you?

A: 45 years

Q: Sir, What is your IQ?

A: Well, I can see pretty well, I think.

Q: Did you blow your horn or anything?

A: After the accident?

Q: Before the accident?

A: Sure, I played for ten years. I even went to school for it.

Q: So the date of conception (of the baby) was August 8th?

A: Yes.

Q: What were you doing at the time?

Q: Is your appearance here this morning pursuant to a deposition notice, which I sent to your attorney?

A: No, this is how I dress when I go to work.

Q: What was the first thing your husband said to you when he woke that morning?

A: He said, "Where am I, Cathy?"

Q: And why did that upset you?

A: My name is Susan.

Q: And where was the location of the accident?

A: Approximately milepost 499.

Q: And where is milepost 499?

A: Probably between milepost 498 and 500.

Q: Do you know if your daughter has ever been involved in voodoo or the occult?

A: We both do.

Q: Voodoo?

A: We do.

Q: You do?

A: Yes, voodoo.

Q: Trooper, when you stopped the defendant, were your red and blue lights flashing?

A: Yes.

Q: Did the defendant say anything when she got out of her car?

A: Yes, sir.

Q: What did she say?

A: 'What disco am I at?'

Q: Now doctor, isn't it true that when a person dies in his sleep, he doesn't know about it until the next morning?

Q: The youngest son, the twenty-year old, how old is he?

Q: Were you present when your picture was taken?

Q: Was it you or your younger brother who was killed in the war?

Q: Did he kill you?

Q: How far apart were the vehicles at the time of the collision?

Q: You were there until the time you left, is that true?

Q: How many times have you committed suicide?

Q: You say the stairs went down to the basement?

A: Yes.

Q: And these stairs, did they go up also?

Q: She had three children, right?

A: Yes.

Q: How many were boys?

A: None.

Q: Were there any girls?

Q: Mr. Slatery, you went on a rather elaborate honeymoon, didn't you?

A: I went to Europe, Sir.

Q: And you took your new wife?

Q: How was your first marriage terminated?

A: By death.

Q: And by whose death was it terminated?

Q: Can you describe the individual?

A: He was about medium height and had a beard.

Q: Was this a male or a female?

Q: Doctor, how many autopsies have you performed on dead people?

A: All my autopsies are performed on dead people.

Q: All your responses must be oral, OK? What school did you go to?

A: Oral.

Q: Do you recall the time that you examined the body?

A: The autopsy started around 8:30 p.m.

Q: And Mr. Dennington was dead at the time?

A: No, he was sitting on the table wondering why I was doing an autopsy.

Q: Are you qualified to give a urine sample?

Q: Doctor, before you performed the autopsy, did you check for a pulse?

A: No.

Q: Did you check for blood pressure?

A: No.

Q: Did you check for breathing?

A: No.

Q: So, then it is possible that the patient was alive when you began the autopsy?

A: No.

Q: How can you be so sure, Doctor?

A: Because his brain was sitting on my desk in a jar.

Q: But could the patient have still been alive nevertheless?

A: It is possible that he could have been alive and practicing law.

BAR JOKES:

A man approached a woman in a bar and said, "Would you like to dance?" She answered, "No!" He said, "You must not have heard what I said!" She said, "Sure I did, you said, "Would you like to dance!" He said, "No, I said that you look fat in those pants!"

A man approached a woman in a bar and said, "Would you like to dance?" She answered, "No!" He said, "Shouldn't be so picky, God knows I wasn't!"

A fellow was at the bar with his brother. He commented that nobody would dance with him and what he could do to remedy the situation. His brother suggested that he put a banana down his pants. After about a half hour he came back and told his brother that it wasn't working. His brother said, "In the front dummy, in the front!"

A guy walks into a bar and sits down next to this good-looking girl and starts looking at his watch. The girl notices this and asks him if his date is late. "No", he replies, "I've just got this new state-of-the-art watch and I was just about to test it." "What does it do?" "It uses alpha waves to telepathically talk to me." "What's it telling you now?" "Well, it says you're not wearing any panties." "Ha! Well it must be broken then 'cuz I am wearing panties!" "Damn thing, must be an hour fast."

A man was sitting at the bar and the bartender asked if he wanted a drink. He ordered a beer and the bartender turned to the man sitting next to him and said, "Hey jackass, you want a beer?" This kind of shocked the man but he sat and finished his beer.

A few minutes later the bartender came back around and asked if he wanted another beer, he ordered and then the bartender asked the man sitting next to him, for the second time, "Hey jackass, you want a beer!" The man ordered another. Puzzled with this type of display, he leaned toward the man and said, "Why would you patronize a place like this? I wouldn't go anywhere that I was called a jackass!" The patron leaned over to the man and said, "Ah, he aw, he aw, he always calls me that!

A drunk gets up from the bar and heads for the bathroom. A few moments later a loud, blood curdling scream is heard coming from the bathroom. A few minutes after that, another loud scream reverberates through the bar. The bartender goes to the bathroom door to investigate why the drunk is screaming. "What's all the screaming about in there?" he yells. "You're scaring the customers," "I'm just sitting here on the toilet," slurs the drunk, "and every time I try to flush, something comes up and squeezes the hell out of my testicles!" With that, the bartender opens the door and says, "You idiot! You're sitting on the mop bucket!!"

A man was sitting at the bar, and after a few drinks, told the bartender that he wanted to buy everyone in the place a drink, including that douche bag over on the other side of the bar. The bartender told him that he appreciated the gesture but said that the lady was a good patron and asked the man to refrain from using such offensive language. Then he proceeded to give everyone a drink. The man finished his drink and again said to the bartender that he wished to buy everybody in the place a drink as well as that Douche bag over on the other side of the bar.

The bartender was a little perturbed and again thanked the man but insisted that he did not use offensive language like that again, then proceeded to give everyone a drink. When he came to the lady at the other end of the bar he apologized for the offense and said, "He did offer to buy you a drink! What would you like?" The lady pondered for a moment and then said, "Vinegar and water!"

A man walked up to the bartender and said that he wanted to make a bet with him. The bartender said, "On what?" He said, "I'll bet you $500.00 that I can stand at one end of the bar and you can put a shot glass at the other end of the bar and I will take a leak and not spill a drop on the bar!" The bartender said, "You gotta deal!" So the man got up and proceeded to piss all over the bar, got down, paid the bartender the $500.00. The bartender was smiling as he cleaned up the mess. When the man started to walk away, the bartender said, "Why would you make such a foolish bet and throw away $500.00?"

To that the man replied, "See that fellow over there at the table?" The bartender said, "Yes!" He said, "Well I just bet him that I could stand up here and piss all over your bar and you would smile as you were wiping it up!"

A man walked into a bar one day and sat there crying in his beer. The bartender said, "Hey Joe, what's the problem." The man replied, "Ah, I don't want to talk about it." The bartender said, "You know Joe, I've been your friend for years and that's what I'm here for so tell me." Joe replied, "Well, I don't know. I just wrote one of the most beautiful love songs anyone could ever hope to write." The bartender replied, "Great! You should be proud of yourself!" Joe said, "Yaw, but nobody's buying it." The bartender inquired, "Why?" He said, "I don't know."

The bartender said, "Well Joe, you play it on the piano, don't you?" Joe replied, "Yes." The bartender said, "Well the band is going to take a break in just a few minutes, why don't you get up and play it?"

Joe consented and in just a few minutes he sat and played the piece. The music and lyrics were so touching that several at the bar, including the bartender, were choked up with tears in their eyes. The bartender said, "Joe that was beautiful. I usually don't get emotional about music but that was touching. He continued, "What did you name it?" Joe said, "I named it (I love you so friggin much I could just shit!)" The bartender replied, "Well there's your problem." Joe said, "What!" The bartender replied, "Titles too long!"

A very short man sat beside a husky-looking fellow in a bar and ordered a drink. In just a few minutes time the big, husky fellow swung his forearm around and knocked the short fellow on the floor and then said, "That's Karate from Korea." The little fellow, speechless, got up, dusted himself off and sat back down. In just a few short minutes the husky fellow swung his elbow and again knocked the short fellow off his seat on his can. Then the husky fellow said, "That's Judo from Japan." The little fellow got up, dusted himself off and left. About a half hour later the little fellow walked up to the bar and cold cocked the big guy, then told the bartender, "Say, when that guy wakes up tell him that that was a crowbar from Sears."

A nude woman walked into a bar one day, walked up to the bar and ordered a drink. The bartender said, "That's fine but how do you expect to pay for it?" She then turned around and bent over. The bartender scratched his head and pondered for a moment, then said "You wouldn't have anything a little smaller, would you?"

An ugly woman walked into a bar with a parakeet on her finger and sat down. There were no women at the bar accept her but several men were sitting around looking at her. She said, "If anyone can guess the weight of the parakeet, I will give them a free piece of ass!" One of the men from the opposite side of the bar looked at her and said, rather sarcastically, 'Fifty pounds!' She looked back and said, "Close enough!"

A man walks into a bar sits down and say, "Bartender, got any specials today?" Bartender says, "Yes, we have mixture of Pabst Blue Ribbon and Smirnoff Vodka." Man says, "Damn, what the hell is that?" Bartender says, "Well we call it a 'Pabst Smir'

A drunk phoned police to report that thieves had been in his car. "They've stolen the dashboard, the steering wheel, the brake pedal, even the accelerator!" he cried out. The police were dumbfounded and dispatched an officer to the scene. However, before the police arrived, the phone rang a second time with the same voice came over the line. "Never mind," he said with a hiccup, "I got in the back seat by mistake."

A police recruit was asked during the exam, "What would you do if you had to arrest your own mother?" He said, "Call for backup."

Two buddies, Jeff and Steve, are getting very drunk at a bar when suddenly Jeff throws up all over himself. "Oh, no, Jane will kill me!" Steve says, "Don't worry, pal. Just tuck a twenty in your breast pocket and tell Jane that someone threw up on you and gave you twenty dollars for the dry cleaning bill." So they stay for another couple hours and get even drunker.

Eventually Jeff rolls into home and his Jane starts to give him a bad time. "You reek of alcohol and you puked all over yourself! My God you are disgusting!" Speaking very carefully so as not to slur, Jeff says "Now wainaminit, I can e'splain everything! Itsh not what you thinks, I only had a couple drinks! But this other guy got sick on me...He'd had one too many and couldn't hold his liquor! He said he was sorry an' gave me twenty bucks for the cleaning bill! "Jane looks in his breast pocket and says "But this is forty dollars!" "Oh yea..." says Jeff. "I almost forgot! He pooped in my pants too!"

A woman is shopping in the local supermarket. She selects some milk, some eggs, a carton of juice, and a package of bacon. As she unloads her items at the cash register to pay, a drunk standing behind her in line watches her place the four items on the belt and states with assurance, "You must be single?" The woman looks at the four items on the belt, and seeing nothing unusual about her selection says, "That's right! How on earth did you know?!" He replies, "Because you're uglier 'n shit!"

A man was sitting next to another man and talking about picking up women. One man said that he knew a good method of doing so. The other man inquired, "How?" He replied, I just sit next to a good-looking woman and kind of mumble, "Tickle your ass with my feather!" If she replies, "Okay," then we go but if she acts astonished and say "What?" I reply, "Particularly nasty weather!"

The other man replied, "I think I'll try that!" After quite a few drinks of liquid courage, he decided to make his proposition and sat next to a good-looking lady. He decided that it was about time to implement his new plan and said, slurring his words, "Stick my feather up your ass!" 'What?' she replied. The man, rather intoxicated, replied, "Ain't the weather a bitch?"

A man was sitting next to a woman at the bar and said, "Would you have sex with me for a million bucks?" She said, 'For a million bucks I suppose I would!' He said, "How about twenty bucks?" She said, 'Wait a minute, you said a million bucks, what do you think I am, a slut?' He said, "Oh, we've already established that, now we're negotiating.

Two men were setting out a bar. One was well off and in his business suit sipping on a martini. The other man, noticeably a blue-collar worker was sitting there drinking a beer. After a few minutes the blue color worker started up conversation with the man in the suit who, in the conversation shared that it was his wife's birthday and he had just been shopping for her. The blue collar worker said, "That's ironic, it is my wife's birthday also." He then asked the rich man what he had given his wife for her birthday and he replied that he bought her a 5 Krt. diamond ring and a Rolls Royce.

The blue collar worker said, "Man, I can see the diamond ring but why the Rolls?" The rich man said, 'Well it seemed like the thing to do at the time, if she doesn't like the ring she can take the new Rolls down to the store and exchange it.' Then he asked the blue-collar worker what he got for his wife. He replied, "I got her a pair of tennis shoes and a dildo!" The rich man replied, 'Well, I can see the tennis shoes but why the dildo?' The blue-collar worker said, "Seemed like the thing to do at the time, cause if she doesn't like the tennis shoes she can go fuck herself!"

While the man savored a double martini at the local bar, an attractive woman sat down next to him. The bartender served her a glass of orange juice. The man turned to her and said, "This is a special day. I'm celebrating." "I'm celebrating, too," she replied, clinking glasses with him.

"What are you celebrating?" he asked. "For years I've been trying to have a child," she answered, "Today my gynecologist told me I'm pregnant!" "Congratulations," the man said, lifting his glass. "As it happens, I'm a chicken farmer, and for years all my hens were infertile. But today they're finally fertile." "How did it happen?" she asked. "I switched cocks." "What a coincidence," she said.

A very attractive lady goes up to a bar in a quiet rural pub. She gestures alluringly to the bartender who comes over immediately. When he arrives, she seductively signals that he should bring his face closer to hers. When he does she begins to gently caress his full beard. "Are you the manager?" she asks, softly stroking his face with both hands. "Actually, no," the man replied. "Can you get him for me? I need to speak to him" she says, running her hands beyond his beard and into his hair. "I'm afraid I can't," breathes the bartender. "Is there anything I can do?" "Yes, there is. I need you to give him a message," she continues, running her forefinger across the bartender's lips and slyly popping a couple of her fingers into his mouth and allowing him to suck them gently. "What should I tell him?" the bartender manages to say. "Tell him," she whispers, "there is no toilet paper, hand soap, or paper towels in the ladies room."

DON'T YA JUST LOVE SHOPPING FOR SHOES?

It was opening night at the Orpheum and The Amazing Claude was topping the bill. People came from miles around to see the famed hypnotist do his stuff. As Claude took to the stage, he announced, unlike most stage hypnotists who invite two or three people up onto the stage to be put into a trance, I intend to hypnotize each and every member of this audience." The excitement was almost electric as Claude withdrew a beautiful antique pocket watch from his coat. "I want you each to keep your eye on this antique watch.

It's a very special watch. It's been in my family for six generations." He began to swing the watch gently back and forth while quietly chanting, "Watch the watch, watch the watch, watch, the watch...."

The crowd became mesmerized as the watch swayed back and forth, light gleaming off its polished surface. Hundreds of pairs of eyes followed the swaying watch, until suddenly it slipped from the hypnotist's fingers and fell to the floor, breaking into a hundred pieces. "Shit!" said the hypnotist. It took three weeks to clean up the theater.

Two drunks were in a tavern sitting at the bar and staring into their drinks. One got a curious look on his face and asked, "Hey, Pete! Have you ever seen an ice cube with a hole in it before?" "Yep, replied the Pete, been married to one for fifteen years."

This man was sitting at the bar and ordered a stiff drink, downed it and looked in his shirt pocket. Ordered another drink and looked again, still another and another and each time looked in his shirt pocket. The bartender, noticing this after about seven drinks asked the man, "Why do you keep looking into your pocket after you down every drink". The man replied, "Well, I have a picture of my wife in that pocket. When she starts looking cute I go home!"

A fellow came into a bar one day and said to the bartender, "Give me six double vodkas!" The bartender said, 'Wow! You must have had one heck of a day!' "Yes," replied the man, "I've just found out my older brother is gay." The next day the same man comes in again and asks for the same drinks. When the bartender asked what the problem was today the answer came back, "I've just found out that my younger brother is gay too!" On the third day the man came into the bar and ordered another six double vodkas. The bartender said, 'Man, doesn't anybody in your family like women?' "Yes," the man replied, "My wife!"

A gay man, finally deciding he could no longer hide his sexuality from his parents, went over to their house, and found his mother in the kitchen cooking dinner. He sat down at the kitchen table, let out a big sigh, and said, "Mom, I have something to tell you: "I'm gay."

His mother made no reply or gave any response, and the guy was about to repeat it to make sure she'd heard him, when she turned away from the pot she was stirring and said calmly, "You're gay -- doesn't that mean you put other men's penises in your mouth?"

The guy said nervously, "Uh, yeah, Mom, that's right." His mother went back to stirring the pot, then suddenly whirled around, whacked him over the head with her spoon and said, "Don't you EVER complain about my cooking again!!!!!"

There once was a successful rancher who died and left everything to his devoted wife. She was determined to keep the ranch and make a go of it but she knew very little about ranching, so she decided to place an ad in the newspaper for ranch hands and two men applied for the job. One was gay and the other a drunk. She thought long and hard about it, and when no one else applied, she decided to hire the gay guy, figuring it would be safer to have him around the house than the drunk.

He turned out to be a fantastic worker, worked long hard hours every day and knew a lot about ranching. For weeks the two of them worked, and the ranch was doing really well.

Then one day the rancher's wife said to the hired hand, "You have done a really good job and we've both done nothing but work for weeks. The ranch looks great, and I'm taking Saturday night off and going into town to kick up my heels and paint the town red, and I think you should do the same."

The hired hand agreed readily, and Saturday night each went to town. The rancher's wife had dinner and drinks with friends, and talked and joked and danced, and had a great time, getting home about midnight. The hired hand wasn't home yet, so she decided to wait up for him. One o'clock and no hired hand yet. Two o'clock and no hired hand and she began to worry. At two-thirty in came the hired hand.

The rancher's wife was sitting by the fireplace and called him over by her "Now I'm the boss", she said, "and you have to do what I tell you, right?" "Well yes", he answered. "Then unbutton my blouse and take it off", she said.

He did as she asked. "Now take off my boots." He did. "Now take off my socks." He did. "Now take off my skirt." He did. "Now take off my bra." Again he did as she asked. "Now take off my panties. And again he did what she told him. Then she looked at him and said, "And don't ever wear my clothes to town again."

This guy goes to a bar located at the top of the Empire State Building in NYC. It looks like a nice place and he seat at the bar next to another guy. "This is a nice place. I've never been here." The first guys says. "Oh, really?" The other replies, "It's also a very special bar." "Why is that?" the first guy asks. "Well you see that painting on the far wall? That's an original Van Gogh and this stool I'm sitting on was on the Titanic." "Gee, that's amazing!" the first guy says. "Not only that, but you see that window over there, fourth from the right? Well, the wind does strange things outside that window. If you jump out you'll fall about 50 feet before the wind catches you and you're pushed back up." "No way, that's impossible," the first guy replies. "Not at all, take a look." the other man replies and walks over to the window followed closely by the first man. He opens the window, climbs over the sill and falls out.

He drops 10...20...30...40...50 feet, then he comes to a stop and whoosh! He comes right back up and sails back through a window. "See, it's fun & You should try it," he says. "Try it? I don't even believe I saw it!" the first man shouts. "It's easy. Watch. I'll do it again." And with that, he falls out the window again. He drops 10...20...30...40...50 feet, comes to an abrupt stop and whoosh! He comes right back up and sails back through a window. "Go ahead, give it a try, it's a blast," he says. "Well what the heck. OK, I'll give it a try," the first man says and proceeds to fall out of the window. He falls 10... 20... 30... 40... 50... 100... 200... 300... 400... 500. 1000 feet and SPLAT, and then ends up as road pizza on the sidewalk below.

After calmly watching the first man fall to his death, the other guy casually closes the window and heads back to the bar and orders, then another drink. The bartender arrives with the drink and says, "You know, Superman, you're a real asshole when you're drunk."

A guy goes into a bar and buys 2 drinks. He downs one, and pours the other all over his hand. What are you doing?" asks the bartender. "Getting my date drunk" he replies.

An Irishman, an Italian, and a Polish guy are in a bar. They are having a good time and all agree that the bar is a nice place. Then the Irishman says, "Aye, this is a nice bar, but where I come from, back in Dublin, there's a better one. At MacDougal's, you buy a drink, you buy another drink, and MacDougal himself will buy your third drink!" The others agree that sounds like a nice place.

Then the Italian says, "Yeah, that's a nice bar, but where I come from, there's a better one. Over in Brooklyn, there's this place, Vinny's. At Vinny's, you buy a drink, Vinny buys you a drink. You buy anudda drink, Vinny buys you anudda drink." Everyone agrees that sounds like a great bar.

Then the Polish guy says, "You think that's great? Where I come from there's this place called Warshowski's. At Warshowski's, they buy you your first drink, they buy you your second drink, they buy you your third drink, and then, they take you in the back and get you laid!" "Wow!" say the other two. "That's fantastic! Did that actually happen to you?" "No," replies the Polish guy, "but it happened to my sister!"

One night a police officer was staking out a particularly rowdy bar, for possible violations of the driving-under-the-influence laws. At closing time, he saw a guy stumble out of the bar, trip on the curb and try his keys on five different cars before he found his. Then he sat in the front seat fumbling around with his keys for several minutes.

The man was so drunk that everyone else left the bar and drove off before he had even put the keys in the ignition. Finally, he started his engine and began to pull away. Chuckling at the pathetic driver, the police officer stopped him, read him his rights and administered the Breathalyzer test. The results showed a reading of 0.0. The puzzled officer demanded to know how this could be. The driver replied, "Tonight I'm the designated decoy."

A woman was shopping at her local supermarket, where she selected a quart of milk, a carton of eggs, juice, and a package of bacon. As she was unloading her items on the conveyer belt to check out, a drunk standing behind her, watched as she placed her items in front of the cashier.

He said, "You must be single." The woman, a bit startled, looked at her four items on the belt, and seeing nothing particularly unusual about her selections said, "Well, ya know, that's right. But how on earth did you know that? The drunk said, "Cause you're uglier 'n hell."

A drunk went into a telephone booth and dialed at random. "Salvation Army," was the answer. "What do you do?" asked the man. "We save wicked men and women," came the reply. "Okay, save me a wicked woman for Saturday night."

THE FIVE STAGES OF DRUNKENNESS:

Stage #1 -- Smart

This is when you suddenly become an expert on every subject. You know all and greatly wish to express this knowledge to anyone who will listen. At this stage you are also always right. And of course the person you are talking with is very wrong. You will talk for hours trying to convince someone that you are right. This makes for an interesting argument when both parties are "smart". Two people talking, in fact, arguing about a subject neither one really knows anything about but are convinced that they are the complete authority on the subject makes for great entertainment for those who get the opportunity to listen in.

Stage #2 -- Handsome/Pretty

This is when you are convinced that you are the best looking person in the entire room and everyone is looking at you. You begin to wink at perfect strangers and ask them to dance because of course they had been admiring you the whole evening. You are the center of attention, and all eyes are directed at you because you are the most beautiful thing on the face of the earth. Now keep in mind that you are still smart, so you can talk to this person who has been admiring you about anything under the sun.

Stage #3 -- Rich

This is when you suddenly become the richest person in the world. You can buy drinks for the entire bar and put it on your bill because you surely have an armored truck full of your money parked behind the bar. You can also make bets in this stage. Now of course you still know all, so you will always win all your bets. And you have no concern for how much money you bet because you have all the money in the world. You will also begin to buy drinks for all the people in the bar who are admiring you because you are now the smartest, most handsome, and richest person on the face of the earth.

Stage #4 -- Bulletproof

You can now pick fights with the people you have been betting money with because you cannot be hurt by anything. At this point you would go up to the boyfriend of the woman who had been admiring your beautiful self all evening and challenge him to a battle of wits for money. You have no worry about losing this battle of wits because you know it all, have all the money to cover this bet, and you will obviously win a fight that might erupt if he loses.

Stage #5-- Invisible

This is the final stage of drunkenness. At this point you can do absolutely anything because no one can see you. You can get up and dance on a table, to impress the people who have been admiring you all evening, because the rest of the people in the room cannot see you. You are also invisible to the person whom you have picked a fight with earlier in the evening. You can walk through the streets singing at the top of your lungs (because of course you are still smart and know the tune perfectly) and no one will think anything of it because they can't see you. All your social inhibitions are gone. You can do anything, because no one will know. And you certainly won't remember.

Bar Room Translations:

1. "You get this one, next round is on me."

   (We won't be here long enough to get another round.)

2. "I'll get this one, next one is on you."

   (Happy hour is about to end...drafts are now a dollar, but by the next round they'll be $4.50 a   pop.)

3. "Hey, where is that friend of yours?"

   (I have no interest in talking to you except as a way to get your attractive friend into a compromising position.)

4. "Can I get a glass of white zinfandel." (female)

   (I'm easy.)

5. "Can I get a glass of white zinfandel." (male)

   (I'm gay.)

6. "Ever try a body shot?" (male to female)

   (I am even willing to drink tequila if it means that I get to lick you.)

7. "Ever try a body shot?" (female to male)

   (If this is how wild I am in the bar, imagine what I'll do to you on the ride home?)

8. "I don't feel well, let's go home." (female)

   (You are paying more attention to your friends than me.)

9. I don't feel well, let's go home." (male)

(I'm horny.)

10. "Who's got the next round?"

(I haven't bought a round in almost 3 years, but I am an expert at diverting attention.)

11. "Excuse Me." (male to male)

(Get the hell out of the way.)

12. "Excuse Me." (male to female)

(I am going to grope you now.) (Editor's Note - one of my personal favorites)

13. "Excuse Me." (female to male)

(Don't even think about groping me, just get the hell out of the way.)

14. "Excuse Me." (female to female)

(Move your fat ass. Who do you think you are anyway? You are not all that, missy, and don't think for one minute that you are. Coming in here dressing like a ho... Get your eyes off of my man, or I'll slap you, bitch, like the slut you are.)

15. "What do you have on tap?"

(What's cheap?)

16. "Can I have a white Russian?" (male)

(I'm *really* gay.)

17. "Can I have a white Russian?" (female)

    (I'm *really* easy.)

18. "That person looks really familiar."

    (Did I sleep with him/her?)

19. Can I just get a glass of water?" (female)

(I'm annoying, but cute enough to get away with this.)

20. I don't have my ID on me." (female)

    (I'm 19.)

21. "I don't have my ID on me." (male)

    (I don't have a license since I got pulled over and blew a 0.15 after my last visit here)

For those tired of the usual "friend" poems, a touch of reality:

When you are sad, I will get you drunk and help you plot revenge against the scum-sucking bastard who made you sad.

When you are blue, I'll try to dislodge whatever's choking you.

When you smile, I'll know you finally got laid.

When you are scared, I will rag you about it every chance I get.

When you are worried, I will tell you horrible stories about how much worse it could be and to quit whining.

When you are confused, I will use little words to explain it to your dumb ass.

When you are sick, Stay away from me until you're well again, I don't want whatever you have.

When you fall, I will point and laugh at your clumsy ass.

This is my oath, I pledge till the end.

Why you may ask?   Because you're my friend.

There was this party in the woods and all of a sudden there was a down pour of thunder and rain. These two men ran for about 10 minutes in the pouring rain, finally reaching their car just as the rain let up. They jumped in the car, started it up and headed down the road, laughing and, of course, still drinking one beer after the other.

All of a sudden an old Indian man's face appeared in the passenger window and tapped lightly on the window! The passenger screamed out, "Eeeekkk! Look at my window!!! There's an old Indian guy's face there!" (Was this a ghost?) This old Indian man kept knocking, so the driver said, "Well open the window a little and ask him what he wants!" So the other guy rolled his window down part way and said, scared out of his wits asks,"What do you want?"

The old Indian softly replied, "You have any tobacco?" The passenger, terrified, looked at the driver and said, "He wants tobacco!" "Well offer him a cigarette! HURRY!!" the driver replies. So he fumbles around with the pack and hands the old man a cigarette and yells, "Step on it!" rolling up the window in terror.

Now going about 80 miles an hour, they calm down and they start laughing again, and the passenger says, "What do you think of that?" The driver says, "I don't know? How could that be? I am going pretty fast?"

Then all of a sudden AGAIN there is a knock on the window and there is the old Indian man again. "Aaaaaaaaaaaah, there he is again!," the passenger yells. "Well, see what he wants now!" yells back the driver. He rolls down the window a little ways and shakily says "Yes?" "Do you have a light?" the old Indian quietly asks. The passenger throws a lighter out the window at him and rolls up the window and yells, "STEP ON IT!"

They are now going about 100 miles an hour and still guzzling beer, trying to forget what they had just seen and heard, when all of a sudden again there is more knocking! "Oh my God, HE'S BACK!" The passenger rolls down the window and screams out, "WHAT DO YOU WANT?" in stark fear. The old man gently replied, "Do you want some help getting out of the mud?"

This is purported to be true:

When NASA was preparing for the Apollo Project, they did some astronaut training on a Navajo Indian Reservation in Arizona.

One day, a Navajo Elder and his son were herding sheep and came across the space crew. The old man, who spoke only Navajo, asked a question which his son translated. "What are these guys in the big suits doing?" A member of the crew said they were practicing for their trip to the Moon. The old man got all excited and asked if he could send a message to the Moon with the astronauts. Recognizing a promotional opportunity for the spin-doctors, the NASA folks found a tape recorder.

After the old man recorded his message, they asked the son to translate it. He refused. So the NASA reps brought the tape to the reservation where the rest of the tribe listened and laughed but refused to translate the Elder's message to the Moon. Finally, the NASA crew called in an official government translator. He reported that the Moon message said, "Watch out for these bastards: they have come to steal your land."

Book Titles:

Under the Bleachers
        by Seymour Butts

Trails in the Sand
        by Peter Dragon

50 Yards to the Outhouse
        by Willie Make it, Betty Won't and illustrated
by Andy Didn't.

Raped in a Gas Station
        by Who-pumped Ethel

Antlers in the Treetops
        by Who Goosed the Moose

Rusty Bedsprings
        by I.P. Nightly

Yellow River
        by I.P. Freely

Holes in the Mattress
        by Mr. Completely

Clergy Humor:

One of the most difficult tasks that a church faces is choosing a good minister. A member on a church board that was involved in this process finally lost his patience. He had watched the Pastoral Selection Committee reject applicant after applicant for some fault, alleged or otherwise. It was time for a bit of soul-searching on the part of the committee. So he stood up and read a letter purporting to be from another applicant.

"Gentlemen: I understand that your pulpit is vacant and would like to apply for the position. I have many qualifications. I've been a preacher with much success and also some success as a writer. Some say that I'm a good organizer. I've been a leader in most of the places I have been."

"I'm over 50 years of age and have never preached in one place for more than three years. In some places I have left town after my work has caused riots and disturbances. I must admit that I have been in jail three or four times, but not because of any wrongdoing. My health is not too good, though I still get a great deal done. The churches I have preached in have been small, though located in several large cities. I've not got along well with religious leaders in towns where I have preached. In fact, some have threatened me and even attacked me physically. I am not too good at keeping records. I have been known to forget whom I have baptized. However, if you can use me, I will do my best for you."

The board member looked over the committee. "Well, what do you think? Shall we call him?"

The board members were shocked. "Call an unhealthy, trouble-making, absent-minded ex-jailbird? Was the board member crazy? "Who signed that application and has such a profound nerve as this?"

The board member eyed them all keenly before he answered. "It's signed, "The Apostle Paul."

Over the massive front doors of a church, these words were inscribed: "The Gate of Heaven". Below that was a small cardboard sign which read: "Please use other entrance."

Rev. Warren J. Keating, Pastor of the First Presbyterian Church of Yuma, AZ, says that the best prayer he ever heard was: "Lord, please make me the kind of person my dog thinks I am."

A Woman went to the Post Office to buy stamps for her Christmas cards. "What Denomination?" Asked the clerk. "Oh, good heavens! Have we come to this?" said the woman. "Well give me 50 Baptist, and 50 Catholic ones."

On a very cold, snowy Sunday in February, only the pastor and one farmer arrived at the village church. The pastor said, "Well, I guess we won't have a service today." The farmer replied: "Heck, if even only one cow shows up at feeding time, I feed it."

During a children's sermon, Rev. Larry Eisenberg asked the children what "Amen" means. A little boy raised his hand and said: "It means "Tha-tha-tha-that's all folks!"

A student was asked to list the Commandments in any order. His answer? "3, 6, 1, 8, 4, 5, 9, 2, 10, 7."

A couple lived near the ocean and used to walk the beach a lot. One summer they noticed a girl who was at the beach pretty much every day. She wasn't unusual, nor was the travel bag she carried, except for one thing; she would approach people who were sitting on the beach, glance around furtively, then speak to them.

Generally the people would respond negatively and she would wander off, but occasionally someone would nod and there would be a quick exchange of money and something she carried in her bag. The couple assumed she was selling drugs, and debated calling the cops, but since they did not know for sure they just continued to watch her.

After a couple of weeks, the wife said, "Honey, have you ever noticed that she only goes up to people with boom boxes and other electronic devices?" He hadn't and said so. Then she said, "Tomorrow I want you to get a towel and our big radio and go lie out on the beach. Then we can find out what she's really doing."

Well, the plan went off without a hitch and the wife was almost hopping up and down with anticipation when she saw the girl talk to her husband and then leave. The man walked up the beach and met his wife at the road. "Well, Is she selling drugs?" she asked excitedly. "No, she's not," he said, enjoying this probably more than he should have. "Well, what is it, then? What does she do?" his wife fairly shrieked. The man grinned and said, "She's a battery salesperson." "Batteries?" cried the wife. "Yes," he replied. She sells C cells down by the Sea Shore.

I was at the beach with my children when my four-year-old son ran up to me, grabbed my hand, and led me to the shore, where a sea gull lay dead in the sand. "Mommy, what happened to him?" the little boy asked. "He died and went to Heaven," I replied. My son thought a moment and then said, "And God threw him back down?"

The Lost Chapter of Genesis

Adam was hanging around the Garden of Eden feeling very lonely. So God asked him, "What's wrong with you?" Adam said he didn't have anyone to talk to. God said that He was going to make Adam a companion and that it would be a woman.

He said, "this pretty lady will gather food for you, she will cook for you, and when you discover clothing, she will wash it for you. She will always agree with every decision you make, and she will not nag you and will always be the first to admit she was wrong when you've had a disagreement.

She will praise you! She will bear your children and never ask you to get up in the middle of the night to take care of them. She will never have a headache and will freely give you love and passion whenever you need it."

Adam asked God, "What will a woman like this cost?" God replied, "An arm and a leg." Then Adam asked, "What can I get for a rib?" Of course, the rest is history.... The End is Near!

Father Boudreaux and pastor Thibodeaux were fishing on the side of the road. They thoughtfully made a sign saying "The End is Near! Turn yourself around now before it's too late," and showed it to each passing car.

The people in one car that passed didn't appreciate the sign and shouted at them: "Leave us alone you religious nuts!" All of a sudden the pastors heard a big splash, looked at each other, and Father Boudreaux said. . .

"You think we should just put up a sign that says: 'bridge- out instead?"

Mother Teresa died and went to heaven. God greets her at the Pearly Gates. "Be thou hungry, Mother Teresa?" asks God. "I could eat," Mother Teresa replied. So God opens a can of tuna and reaches for a chunk of rye bread and they share it. While eating this humble meal, Mother Teresa looks down into Hell and sees the inhabitants devouring huge steaks, lobsters, pheasants, pastries, and wines. Curious, but deeply trusting, she remains quiet.

The next day God again invites her to join him for a meal. Again, it is tuna and rye bread. Once again, Mother Teresa can see the demons of Hell enjoying caviar, champagne, lamb, truffles, and chocolates. Still she says nothing. The following day, mealtime arrives & another can of tuna is opened. She can't contain herself any longer. Meekly, she says: "God, I am grateful to be in heaven with you as a reward for the pious, obedient life I led. But here in heaven all I get to eat is tuna and a piece of rye bread and in the Other Place they eat like emperors and kings! I just don't understand, "God sighs. "Let's be honest," he says, "for just two people, does it pay to cook?"

The priest in a small Irish village was very fond of the chickens he kept in the hen house out back of the parish rectory. He had a prized cock rooster and about ten hens. One Saturday night the rooster was missing, and the priest suspected that it had something to do with the cock fights which occurred in the village. So he decided to speak about it at church the next morning at Mass, he asked the congregation, "Has anybody got a cock?" All the men stood up. "No, No," he said, "that wasn't what I meant. Has anybody seen a cock?" All the women stood up. "No, No," he said, "that wasn't what I meant. Has anybody seen a cock that doesn't belong to them?" Half the women stood up. "No, No," he said, "that wasn't what I meant. Has anybody seen my cock?" All the altar boys stood up.

Lost on a rainy night, a nun stumbles across a monastery and requests shelter there. Fortunately, she's just in time for dinner and was treated to the best fish and chips she had ever tasted. After dinner, she went into the kitchen to thank the chefs. She was met by two of the Brothers. The first one says, "Hello, I am Brother Michael, and this is Brother Charles."

"I'm very pleased to meet you," replies the nun. I just wanted to thank you for a wonderful dinner. The fish and chips were the best I've ever had! Out of curiosity, who cooked what?" Brother Charles replied, "Well, I'm the fish friar." She turned to the other Brother and said, "Then you must be...?" "Yes, I'm afraid so--I am the chip monk."

Father O'Malley got up one fine spring day and walked to the window of his bedroom to get a deep breath of the beautiful day outside and noticed there was a jackass lying dead in the middle of his front lawn.

He promptly called the local police station. The conversation went like this:

"Top o' the day to ye. This is Sgt. Flaherty. How might I help ye?" "And the rest of the day to yesef. This is Father O'Malley at St. Brigid's. There's a jackass lying dead in me front lawn. Would ye be after sending a couple o' yer lads to take care of the matter?"

Sgt. Flaherty considered himself to be quite a wit and the rest of the conversation proceeded like this: "Well now father, it was always my impression that you people took care of last rites!" There was dead silence on the line for a moment and then Father O'Malley replied:

"Aye, that's certainly true, but we are also obliged to notify the next of kin!"

If You Love Something:
If you love something, set it free. If it comes back,
it will always be yours. If it doesn't come back, it was never yours
to begin with. But, if it just sits in your living room, messes up your
stuff, eats your food, uses your telephone, takes your money, and
doesn't appear to realize that you had set it free... You either married
it or gave birth to it.

Bill Keane, creator of the Family Circus cartoon strip tells of a time when
he was penciling one of his cartoons and his son Jeffy said, "Daddy, how
do you know what to draw?" I said, "God tells me." Jeffy said, "Then why
do you keep erasing parts of it?"

After the church service, a little boy told the pastor: "When I grow up,
I'm going to give you some money." "Well, thank you," the pastor replied,
"but why?" "Because my daddy says you're one of the poorest preachers
we've ever had."

My wife invited some people to dinner. At the table, she turned to our
six-year-old daughter and said, "Would you like to say the blessing?" "I
wouldn't know what to say," she replied. "Just say what you hear Mommy
say," my wife said. Our daughter bowed her head and said: "Dear Lord,
why on earth did I invite all these people to dinner?"

Little Jimmy was lying about on a hillside in the middle of a meadow on
a warm spring day. Puffy white clouds rolled by and he pondered their
shape. Soon, he began to think about God. "God? Are you really there?"
Jimmy said out loud. To his astonishment a voice came from the clouds.
"Yes, Jimmy? What can I do for you?" Seizing the opportunity, Jimmy
asked, "God? What is a million years like to you?"

Knowing that Jimmy could not understand the concept of infinity, God responded in a manner to which Jimmy could relate. "A million years to me, Jimmy, is like a minute." "Oh," said Jimmy. "Well, then, what's a million dollars like to you?" "A million dollars to me, Jimmy, is like a penny." "Wow!" remarked Jimmy, getting an idea. "You're so generous... can I have one of your pennies?" God replied, "Sure thing, Jimmy! Just a minute."

During the wedding rehearsal, the groom approached the pastor with an unusual offer. "Look, I'll give you $100 if you'll change the wedding vows. When you get to me and the part where I'm to promise to 'love, honor and obey' and 'forsaking all others, be faithful to her forever,' I'd appreciate it if you'd just leave that part out." He passed the minister a $100 bill and walked away satisfied.

It is now the day of the wedding, and the bride and groom have moved to that part of the ceremony where the vows are exchanged. When it comes time for the groom's vows, the pastor looks the young man in the eye and says:

"Will you promise to prostrate yourself before her, obey her every command and wish, serve her breakfast in bed every morning of your life and swear eternally before God and your lovely wife that you will not ever even look at another woman, as long as you both shall live?" The groom gulped and looked around, and said in a tiny voice, "Yes."

After the wedding, the groom pulled the pastor aside and hissed, "I thought we had a deal." The pastor put the $100 bill into the groom's hand and whispered back, "She made me a much better offer."

One Sunday morning, the pastor noticed little Alex was staring up at the large plaque that hung in the foyer of the church. It was covered with names, and small American flags were mounted on either side of it.

The seven-year-old had been staring at the plaque for some time, so the pastor walked up, stood beside the boy and said quietly, "Good morning Alex." "Good morning Pastor," replied the young man, still focused on the plaque. "Pastor McGhee, what is this?" Alex asked. "Well, son, it's a memorial to all the men and women who have died in the service." Soberly, they stood together, staring at the large plaque. Little Alex's voice was barely audible when he asked, "Which one, the 9:00 or the 10:30 service?"

A businessman was in a great deal of trouble. His business was failing, he had put everything he had into the business, he owed everybody-- it was so bad he was even contemplating suicide. As a last resort he went to a priest and poured out his story of tears and woe.

When he had finished, the priest said, "Here's what I want you to do, put a beach chair and your Bible in your car and drive down to the beach. Take the beach chair and the Bible to the water's edge, sit down in the beach chair, and put the Bible in your lap. Open the Bible; the wind will rifle the pages, but finally the open Bible will come to rest on a page. Look down at the page and read the first thing you see. That will be your answer, that will tell you what to do."

A year later the businessman went back to the priest and brought his wife and children with him. The man was in a new custom-tailored suit, his wife in a mink coat, the children shining. The businessman pulled an envelope stuffed with money out of his pocket, gave it to the priest as a donation in thanks for his advice.

The priest recognized the benefactor, and was curious. "You did as I suggested?" he asked. "Absolutely," replied the businessman. "You went to the beach?" "Absolutely." "You sat in a beach chair with the Bible in your lap?" "Absolutely." "You let the pages rifle until they stopped?" "Absolutely." "And what were the first words you saw?" "Chapter 11," he replied.

A Baptist preacher and his wife decided they needed a dog. Ever mindful of the congregation, they knew the dog must also be Baptist. They visited an expensive kennel and explained their needs to the manager, who assured them he had just the dog for them. The dog was produced and the manager said "Fetch the Bible." The dog bounded to the bookshelf, scrutinized the books, located the Bible, and brought it to the manager. The manager then said "Find Psalms 23."

The dog, showing marvelous dexterity with his paws, leafed thru the Bible, found the correct passage, and pointed to it with his paw. Duly impressed, the couple purchased the dog.

That evening a group of parishioners came to visit. The preacher and his wife began to show off the dog, having him locate several Bible verses. The visitors were amazed. Finally, one man asked "Can he do normal dog tricks too?" "Let's see," said the preacher. Pointing his finger at the dog, he commanded "Heel The dog immediately jumped up on a chair, placed one paw on the preacher's forehead and began to howl. The preacher turned to his wife and exclaimed," Good grief, we've bought a Pentecostal dog!"

One day God was looking down at Earth and saw all of the evil that was going on. He decided to send an angel down to Earth to check it out. So he called on a female angel and sent her to Earth for a time. When she returned she told God, yes it is bad on Earth, 95% is bad and 5% is good.

Well, he thought for a moment and said maybe I had better send down a male angel; to get both points of view. So God called a male angel and sent him to Earth for a time. When the male angel returned he went to God and told him yes, the Earth was in decline, 95% was bad and 5% was good. God said this was not good. He decided to E-mail the 5% that were good and encourage them, a little something to help them keep going. Do you know what that E-mail said? Oh! You didn't get one either?

Most people assume WWJD is for "What would Jesus do?" But the initials really stand for "What would Jesus drive?" One theory is that Jesus would tool around in an old Plymouth because the Bible says, "God drove Adam and Eve out of the Garden of Eden in a Fury." But in Psalm 83, the Almighty clearly owns a Pontiac and a Geo--the passage urges Jesus to "pursue your enemies with your Tempest and terrify them with your Storm." Perhaps God favors Dodge pickup trucks because Moses' followers are warned not to go up a mountain "until the Ram's horn sounds a long blast." Some scholars insist that Jesus drove a Honda but didn't like to talk about it. As proof they cite a verse in St. John's gospel where Christ tells the crowd, "...for I did not speak of my own Accord." Meanwhile, Moses rode an old British motorcycle, as evidenced by a Bible passage declaring that "the roar of Moses' Triumph is heard in the hills." Joshua drove a Triumph sports car with a hole in the muffler--"Joshua's Triumph was heard throughout the land." And following Jesus' lead, the Apostles car pooled in a Honda--"...the Apostles were in one Accord."

A middle-aged woman is in a terrible accident and is rushed to the hospital. On the way there, her vital signs fail. The doctors are able to revive her, but, while she is gone, she sees God and he tells her she has 40 more years to live. Since she is in the hospital, anyway, and knows she's going to be around for a while, she decides to use the stay for self-improvement. She has a face-lift, a fanny-lift, and breast implants. She gets released from the hospital and, as she crosses the street, is run over by a truck and killed. When she sees God again, she says to him, "I thought you said I had 40 years left to live!" To which God replies, "I'm sorry ... I didn't recognize you."

Muldoon lived alone in the Irish countryside with his pet dog for company. One day the dog died, and Muldoon went to the parish priest and asked, "Father, me dog is dead; could ya be sayin a mass for de poor creature?"

Father Patrick replied, "I'm afraid not; we cannot have services for an animal in the church... but there are some Baptists down the lane, and there's jus no tellin what they believe. Maybe they'll do something for the creature."

Muldoon said, "I'll go right away Father; do ya think $5,000 is enough to donate for the service? Father Patrick exclaimed, "Sweet Mary, Mother of Jesus, why didn't ya tell me the dog was Catholic?

Said the elder priest, "I know you were reaching out to the young people when you had bucket seats put in to replace the first four pews. It worked, we got the front of the church filled first." The young priest nodded and the old one continued, "And, you told me a little more beat to the music would bring young people back to church, so I supported you when you brought in that rock'n'roll gospel choir." "So," asked the young priest, "what's the problem?" "Well," said the elder priest, "I'm afraid you've gone too far with the drive-in confessional and the flashing neon sign which reads "Toot'n Tell or Go To Hell"

I Stand at the Door

A new pastor moved into town and went out one Saturday to visit his parishioners. All went well until he came to one house. It was obvious that someone was home, but no one came to the door even after he had knocked several times. Finally, he took out his card, wrote on the back "Revelation 3:20" and stuck it in the door.

The next day, as he was counting the offering he found his card in the collection plate. Below his message was a notation "Genesis 3:10". Revelation 3:20 reads: "Behold, I stand at the door and knock. If any man hear my voice, and opens the door, I will come in to him, and will dine with him, and he will with me." Genesis 3:10 reads: "And he said, I heard thy voice in the garden, and I was afraid, because I was naked."

A man has been in business for many, many years and the business is going down the drain. He is seriously contemplating suicide, and he doesn't know what to do. He goes to the Rabbi to seek his advice. He tells the Rabbi about all of his problems in the business and asks the Rabbi what he should do.

The Rabbi says "Take a beach chair and a Bible and put them in your car and take them down to the edge of the ocean. Go to the water's edge. Take the beach chair out of the car, sit on it, and take the Bible out and open it up. The wind will riffle the pages for a while and eventually the Bible will stay open at a particular page. Read the first words your eyes fall on and they will tell you what to do."

The man does as he is told. He places a beach chair and a Bible in his car and drives down to the beach. He sits on the chair at the water's edge and opens the bible. The wind riffles the pages of the Bible and then stops at a particular page. He looks down at the Bible and his eyes fall on words which tell him what he has to do.

Three months later the man and his family come back to see the Rabbi. The man is wearing a $3,000 Italian suit, The wife is all decked out with a full-length mink coat and the child is dressed in beautiful silk. The man hands the Rabbi a thick envelope full of money and tells him that he wants to donate this money to the synagogue in order to thank the Rabbi for his wonderful advice. The Rabbi is delighted. He recognizes the man and asks him what words in the Bible brought this good fortune to him. The man replies" Chapter 11"

MONEY

It can buy you a House, but not a Home
It can buy you a Bed, but not Sleep
It can buy you a Clock, but not Time
It can buy you a Book, but not Knowledge
It can buy you a Position, but not Respect
It can buy you Medicine, but not Health
It can buy you Blood, but not Life
So you see, money isn't everything. The best things in life can't be bought, and often we destroy ourselves trying! I tell you all this because I am your Friend, and as your Friend I want to take away your needless pain and suffering... So send me all your money and I will suffer for you. No truer Friend than me will you ever find. CASHIER CHECKS ONLY, PLEASE.

"THE POWER OF THE PRESS"

A preacher wanted to raise money for his church and being told that there was a fortune in horse racing decided to purchase one and enter him into a race. However, at the local auction, the going price for horses was so steep that he ended up buying a donkey instead. He figured since he had it he might as well go ahead and enter it in the race. To his surprise, the donkey came in third. The next day the racing sheets carried this headline:

PREACHER'S ASS SHOWS:

The preacher was so pleased with the donkey that he entered it in the race again and this time it won. The paper read:

PREACHER'S ASS OUT IN FRONT:

The Bishop was so upset with this kind of publicity that he ordered the preacher not to enter the donkey in another race. The newspaper printed this headline:

BISHOP SCRATCHES PREACHER'S ASS:

This was too much for the Bishop. He ordered the preacher to get rid of the animal. The preacher decided to give it to a nun in a nearby convent. The headlines the next day read:

NUN HAS BEST ASS IN TOWN:

The Bishop fainted. He informed the nun that she would have to dispose of the donkey. She finally found a farmer who was willing to buy it for ten dollars. The newspaper stated:

NUN PEDDLES ASS FOR TEN DOLLARS:

They Buried the Bishop the next day.

When the Creator was making the world, He called man aside and bestowed upon him 20 years of normal sex life. Man was horrified! "Only 20 years!" he complained. But the Creator didn't budge. That was all He would grant him. Then He called the monkey and gave him 20 years. "But I don't need 20 years," said the monkey, "10 is plenty."

Man spoke up and said, "Can't I have the other 10 years?" The monkey agreed. Then the Creator called the lion and gave him 20 years. The lion said he desired only 10 years. Again, man asked, "Can't I have the other 10 years?" "Of course," roared the lion. Then came the donkey. He, too, was given 20 years and like the others said 10 years was all he needed. Man asked again for the spare 10 years and again received them.

This explains why man has 20 years of normal sex life, 10 years of monkeying around, 10 years of lion about it, and 10 years of making an ass out of themselves.

A boy was sitting on a park bench with one hand resting on an open Bible. He was loudly exclaiming his praise to God. "Hallelujah! Hallelujah! God is great!" he yelled without worrying whether anyone heard him or not.

Shortly after, along came a man who had recently completed some studies at a local university. Feeling himself very enlightened in the ways of truth and very eager to show this enlightenment, he asked the boy about the source of his joy. "Hey" asked the boy in return with a bright laugh, "Don't you have any idea what God is able to do? I just read that God opened up the waves of the Red Sea and led the whole nation of Israel right through the middle."

The enlightened man laughed lightly, sat down next to the boy and began to try to open his eyes to the "realities" of the miracles of the Bible. "That can all be very easily explained. Modern scholarship has shown that the Red Sea in that area was only 10-inches deep at that time. It was no problem for the Israelites to wade across." The boy was stumped. His eyes wandered from the man back to the Bible laying open in his lap. The man, content that he had enlightened a poor, naive young person to the finer points of scientific insight, turned to go.

Scarcely had he taken two steps when the boy began to rejoice and praise louder than before. The man turned to ask the reason for this resumed jubilation. "Wow!" exclaimed the boy happily, "God is greater than I thought! Not only did He lead the whole nation of Israel through the Red Sea, He topped it off by drowning the whole Egyptian army in 10-inches of water!"

GoodWords:There is the story of a person who got up one Sunday and announced to his congregation: "I have good news and bad news. The good news is, we have enough money to pay for our new building program. The bad news is, it's still out there in your pockets."

A Sunday School teacher began her lesson with a question, "Boys and girls, what do we know about God?" A hand shot up in the air. "He is an artist!" said the kindergarten boy. "Really? How do you know?" the teacher asked. "You know - Our Father, who does art in Heaven... "

A minister waited in line to have his car filled with gas just before a long holiday weekend. The attendant worked quickly, but there were many cars ahead of him in front of the service station. Finally, the attendant motioned him toward a vacant pump. "Reverend," said the young man, "Sorry about the delay, it seems as if everyone waits until the last minute to get ready for a long trip." The minister chuckled, "I know what you mean. It's the same in my business."

People want the front of the bus, back of the church and center of attention.

Somebody once figured out that we have 35 million laws trying to enforce 10 commandments.

"Somebody has well said that there are only two kinds of people in the world - there are those who wake up in the morning and say, "Good morning, Lord," and there are those who wake up in the morning and say, "Good Lord, it's Morning!"

A father was approached by his small son, who told him proudly, "I know what the Bible means!" His father smiled and replied, "What do you mean, you 'know' what the Bible means?" The son replied, "I do know!" "Okay," said his father. "So, Son, what does the Bible mean? B -BASIC I - INSTRUCTIONS B - BEFORE L - LEAVING E - EARTH

Clocks in Heaven:

A man passed away and went to heaven. Upon arriving at the pearly gates, St. Peter said, "Come on in. I'll show you around." Walking through the gates, the man noticed that there were clocks everywhere. It appeared that heaven was nothing more than a giant clock warehouse. Surprised at how Heaven looked, the man asked St. Peter, "What's the deal with all the clocks?"

St. Peter replied, "They keep track of everybody on earth. There is one clock for each person. Every time someone tells a lie, his clock moves forward one minute. For instance, this clock belongs to Sam, a used car salesman. If you watch it closely, it will move any second." Click.

The minute hand on Sam's clock moved forward one minute. Click. It moved forward another minute. "Sam must be closing on a deal right now," said St. Peter. "The minute hand on his clock moves all day long.

The man and St. Peter continued walking and soon came across a clock covered with cobwebs. "Whose clock is this?" asked the man. "That clock belongs to the Widow Mary. She is one of the finest persons on earth. I bet her clock hasn't moved in a year or two."

They continued walking and touring Heaven. When the tour was finally finished, the man said, "I've seen everyone's clock but one. Where is the President clock kept?" St. Peter smiled and said, "Look up there. We use his for a ceiling fan."

After many years of illness, Ronald Reagan was very ill and it appeared that he might not pull through. Obviously, Nancy and the rest of the family were at his side, as well as the family minister. Knowing that his time might be short, they asked if there was anything that he wanted. "Yes," he replied, "I'd like very much to have Bill and Hillary Clinton at my side before I go." They were all amazed at this request and several assumed that his memory was failing even worse than they had suspected. Regardless, they went ahead and forwarded his request to the former first family.

Within hours, the former president and first lady arrived at his bedside, via Air Force One which was dispatched by George W for the purpose. For a time, no one said anything. Both Bill and Hillary were touched and flattered that Ron would ask them to be with him during his final moments.

They were also puzzled - they were of different political parties and obviously had thrown barbs in one another's direction over the years. Why not George H Bush Sr.? or George W. Bush, or some of Reagan's many Hollywood friends? He had never given the Clintons any indication that he particularly liked either of them.

Finally, Bill spoke up and asked, "Mr. President, why did you choose the two of us to be at your bedside at this critical moment?" The former president mustered up some strength and said very weakly, "Jesus died between two thieves and that's just exactly how I want to go."

I sat, as did millions of other Americans, and government underwent a peaceful transition of power a year ago last January. At first I felt a swell of pride and patriotism as I watched George W. Bush take his oath of office. However, all that pride vanished as I watched William Jefferson Clinton board Air Force One for the final time. I saw 21 U.S. Marines in full dress with their rifles, fire a 21-gun salute to the outgoing president. It was then that I realized how far America's military had deteriorated. Every last one of them missed.

Letter from the Clinton's to John Hinkley:

January 19, 2001
Mr. John Hinkley
St. Elizabeth Hospital
Washington D.C.

Dear John,

Hillary and I wanted to drop you a short note to tell you how pleased we are with the great strides you are making in your recovery. In our country's new spirit of understanding and forgiveness we want you to know there is a bilateral consensus of compassion and forgiveness abroad throughout the land. Hillary and I want you to know that no grudge is born against you for shooting President Reagan.

We, above all, are aware of how the mental stress and pain could have driven you to such an act of desperation.

As such, as one of my lasts acts as President of the country, I hereby issue you a full pardon and ordered your release from the hospital as soon as possible.

Hillary and I are confident that you will have made complete recovery and that you should return to your family to join the world again as a healthy and productive young man.

Best wishes,

Bill Clinton

P.S. George W is banging Jodie Foster

Why we forward Jokes on email:
This explains it....

"Doesn't it make you mad for them to use your name like that?" "No. I can see how you might think so, but we're just happy that they screen out the folks who'll leave their best friends behind." Soooo... sometimes we wonder why friends keep forwarding jokes to us without writing a word, maybe this could explain: When you are very busy but still want to keep in touch, guess what you do? You forward jokes.

When you have nothing to say, but still want to keep contact, you forward jokes. When you have something to say, but don't know what, and don't know how, you forward jokes. And to let you know that you are still remembered, you are still important, you are still loved, you are still cared for, guess what you get? A forwarded joke!

So my friend, next time if you get a joke, don't think that you've been sent just another forwarded joke, but that you've been thought of today and your friend on the other end of your computer wanted to send you a smile... Have a great day.

How the Internet Began

In ancient Israel, it came to pass that a trader by the name of Abraham Com did take unto himself a young wife by the name of Dot. And Dot Com was a comely woman, broad of shoulder and long of leg. Indeed, she had been called Amazon Dot Com.

She said unto Abraham, her husband: "Why doth thou travel far from town to town with thy goods when thou can trade without ever leaving thy tent?"

And Abraham did look at her as though she were several saddle bags short of a camel load, but simply said: "How, Dear?"

Dot replied, "I will place drums in all the towns and drums in between to send messages saying what you have for sale and they will reply telling you which hath the best price. And the sale can be made on the drums and delivery made by Uriah's Pony Stable (UPS)."

Abraham thought long and decided he would let Dot have her way with the drums. The drums rang out and were an immediate success. Abraham sold all the goods he had at the top price, without ever moving from his tent.

But this success did arouse envy. A man named Maccabi did secret himself inside Abraham's drum and was accused of insider trading. And the young men did take to Dot Com's trading as doth the greedy horseflies take to camel dung.

They were called Nomadic Ecclesiastical Rich Dominican Siderites, or NERDS for short. And lo, the land was so feverish with joy at the new riches and the deafening sound of drums that no one noticed that the real riches were going to the drum maker, one Brother William of Gates, who bought up every drum company in the land. And indeed did insist on making drums that would work only with Brother Gates' drumheads and drumsticks.

Dot did say, "Oh, Abraham, what we have started is being taken over by others." And as Abraham looked out over the Bay of Ezekiel, or as it came to be known "eBay" he said: "We need a name that reflects what we are." And Dot replied, "Young Ambitious Hebrew Owner Operators."

"YAHOO," said Abraham. And that is how it all began. . .

Jesus and Satan were having an argument about who could get the most out of a computer. This had been going on for days and God was tired of hearing all the bickering. God said, "Cool it, guys. I'm setting up a two-hour test to judge who really is the better computer whiz." So, he sat them down at the keyboards and said, "Sic'em."

They did spreadsheets. They wrote reports. They sent faxes. They sent out e-mail. They sent out e-mail with attachments. They downloaded. They did genealogy reports. They made cards. They installed programs. They uninstalled programs. They did every known job.

But just a few minutes before the two hours were up, a bolt of lightning flashed from the sky. The thunder rolled and the rains came down hard. And, in the midst of it all, the electricity went off! Satan was upset, then fumed and fussed, ranted and raved and all to no avail. The electricity stayed off. After a bit, the rains stopped and the electricity came on.

Satan turned to God in desperation, "We lost it all when the power went off! What are we going to do? We'll never know who's the best! That isn't fair!" Jesus grinned. Satan asked Jesus how far he'd gotten into the test. Jesus rebooted his computer, pushed "print" and the printer spewed out the completed test! "How did he do it?" Satan asked God. God smiled and said, "Jesus Saves."

A man walked into the ladies department of Macy's store. He shyly walked up to the woman behind the counter and "I'd like to buy a bra for my wife". "What type of bra?" asked the clerk? "Type?" inquiries the man. "There is more than one type?"

"Look around", said the sales lady, as she showed a sea of bras in every shape, size, color, and material. "Actually, even with all of this variety, there are really only three types of bras" the clerk replied. There is the "Catholic" type, the "Salvation Army" type, and the "Baptist" type. "Which one do you need?"

Still confused, the man asked, "What is the difference between the bras?" The lady responded "It is all quite simple. The Catholic type supports the masses, the Salvation Army type lifts up the fallen, and the Baptist type makes mountains out of mole hills.

A priest and a rabbi are riding in a plane. After a while, the priest turns to the rabbi and asks, "Is it still a requirement of your faith that you do not eat pork?" The rabbi responds, "Yes, that is still one of our beliefs." The priest then asks, "Have you ever eaten pork?" To which the rabbi replies, "Yes, on one occasion I did succumb to temptation and tasted pork." The priest nodded in understanding and went on with his reading.

A while later, the rabbi spoke up and asked the priest, "Father, is it still a requirement of your church that you remain celibate?" The priest replied, "Yes, that is still very much a part of our faith." The rabbi then asked him, "Father, have you ever fallen to the temptations of the flesh?" The priest replied, "Yes Rabbi, on one occasion I was weak and broke with my faith." The rabbi nodded understandingly for a moment and then said, "A lot better than pork, isn't it?"

Two priests were going to Hawaii on vacation and decided that they would make this a real vacation by not wearing anything that would identify them as clergy. As soon as the plane landed, they headed for a store and bought some really outrageous shorts, shirts, sandals, sunglasses, etc. The next morning, they went to the beach, dressed in their "tourist" garb and were sitting on beach chairs, enjoying a drink, the sunshine and the scenery when a "drop dead gorgeous" blonde in a tiny bikini came walking straight towards them.

They couldn't help but stare and when she passed them, smiled and said, "Good morning Father," "Good morning Father," nodding and addressing each of them individually, then passed on by. They were both stunned. How in the world did she recognize them as priests?

The next day they went back to the store, bought even more outrageous outfits -- these were so loud, you could hear them before you even saw them--and again settled on the beach in their chairs to enjoy the sunshine, etc.

After a while, the same gorgeous blonde, wearing a string bikini this time, came walking toward them again. (They were glad they had sunglasses, because their eyes were about to pop out of their heads) Again, she approached them and greeted them individually: "Good morning Father," "Good morning Father," and started to walk away. One of the priests couldn't stand it and said, "Just a minute young lady. Yes, we are priests, and proud of it, but I have to know, how in the world did YOU know?" "Oh Father, don't you recognize me? I'm sister Mary!"

A priest walking down the street notices a young boy on this tiptoes trying to press a doorbell on a house across the street. Although he is trying very hard, the boy is not tall enough to reach the doorbell. After watching the boy's efforts for a moment, the priest walks across the street, up the steps to the porch, comes up behind the little fellow, and lifts him up a couple feet. The boy giggles as he gives the bell a solid ring. Crouching down to the child's level, the priest smiles benevolently and asks, "And now what, my little man?" With a mischievous grin he replies, "Now we run!!!"

A cab driver picks up a nun. She gets into the cab, and the cab driver won't stop staring at her. She asks him, "Why are you staring"? and he replies, "I have a question to ask you, but I don't want to offend you."

She answers, "My dear son, you cannot offend me. When you're as old as I am and have been a nun as long as I have, you get a chance to see and hear just about everything. I'm sure that there's nothing you could say or ask that I would find offensive." "Well, I've always had a fantasy to have a nun kiss me." She responds, "Well, let's see what we can do about that: #1, you have to be single and #2 you must be Catholic."

The cab driver is very excited and says, "Yes, I am single and I'm Catholic too!" The nun says "OK, pull into the next alley." He does and the nun fulfills his fantasy. But when they get back on the road, the cab driver starts crying. "My dear child," said the nun, "why are you crying?"

"Forgive me sister, but I have sinned. I lied, I must confess, I'm married and I'm Jewish." The nun says, "That's OK, my name is Bruce and I'm on my way to a Halloween party."

Sister Mary Katherine lived in a nunnery, a block away from Jack's liquor store. One day, in walked Sister Mary Katherine and she said, "Oh Jack, give me a pint o' the brandy." "Sister Mary Katherine," exclaimed Jack, "I could never do that! I've never sold alcohol to a nun in my life!" "Oh Jack," she responded, "it's only for the Mother Superior." Her voice dropped. "It helps her constipation, you know." So Jack sold her the brandy.

Later that night Jack closed the store and walked home. As he passed the nunnery, who should he see but Sister Mary Katherine. And she was 'wasted'. She was singing and dancing, whirling around and flapping her arms like a bird, right there on the sidewalk. A crowd was gathering so Jack pushed through and exclaimed, "Sister Mary Katherine, for shame! You told me this was for the Mother Superior's constipation!" Sister Mary Katherine didn't miss a beat as she replied: "And so it is, me lad, so it is. When she sees me, she's going to shit!"

"The Nun"

A nun was going to Chicago. She went to the airport and sat down waiting for her flight. She looked over in the corner and saw one of those weight machines that tells your fortune. So, she thought to herself "I'll give it a try just to see what it tells me. "She went over to the machine and put her nickel in, and out came a card that said, "You're a nun, and you weigh 128 lbs. and you are going to Chicago, Ill. She sat back down and thought that it probably tells everyone the same thing, but decided to try it again. She went back to the machine and put her nickel in. Out came a card that read, you're a nun, you weigh 128 lbs. and you're going to Chicago, and you are going to play a fiddle.

The nun said to herself, "I know that's wrong; I have never played a musical instrument in my life." She sat back down and from nowhere a Cowboy came over and set his fiddle case down next to her. The nun picked up the fiddle and started to play beautiful music. Startled, she looked back at the machine and said, "This is incredible. I've got to try it again."

Back to the machine. She put her nickel in and another card came out. It said, "You're a nun, you weigh 128 lbs., you are going to Chicago, and you are going to break wind." Now, she knows the Machine is wrong; I've never broken wind in public in my life!" Well, she tripped and fell off the scales and broke wind. Stunned, she sat back down and looked at the machine. She said to herself, "This is truly unbelievable! I've got to try again."

She went back to the machine, put in her nickel and collected the card. It said, "You're a nun, you still weigh 128 lbs. and you have fiddled and farted around and missed your flight to Chicago!!!!!

If God were process oriented, the book of Genesis would read something like this: In the beginning, God created the heavens and the earth. The earth was without form and void; so God created a small committee. God carefully balanced the committee visa-a-versa race, sex, ethnic origin and economic status in order to interface pluralism with the holistic concepts of self-determination according to adjudicatory guidelines. Even God was impressed, and so ended the first day.

And God said, "Let the Committee draw up a mission statement." And behold, the Committee decided to prioritize and strategize. And God called that process empowerment. And God thought it sounded pretty good. And evening and morning were the second day.

And God said, "Let the Committee determine goals and objectives, and engage in long-range planning." fortunately, a debate as to the semantic differences between goals and objectives pre-empted almost all the third day. Although the question was never satisfactorily resolved, God thought the 'process' was constructive. And evening and morning were the third day.

And God said, "Let there be a retreat in which the Committee can envision functional organization, and engaged in planning, be objective. The Committee considered adjustment of priorities and consequential alternatives to program directions and God saw that this was good. And God thought that is was even worth all the coffee and donuts he had to supply. And so ended the fourth day.

And God said, "Let the Committee be implemented consistent with long-range planning and strategy." The Committee considered guidelines and linkages and structural sensitivities, and alternative and implemental models. And God saw that this was very democratic. And so would have ended the fifth day, except for the unintentional renewal of the debate about the differences between goals and objectives.

On the sixth day, the Committee agreed on criteria for adjudicatory assessment and evaluation. This wasn't the agenda God had planned. He wasn't able to attend, however, because he had to take the afternoon to create day and night, heaven, earth and seas, plants and trees, seasons and years, sun and moon, birds, fish, animals and human beings.

On the seventh day, God rested and the Committee submitted its recommendations. It turned out that the recommended forms for things were nearly identical to the way God had already created them; so the Committee passed a resolution commending God for His implementation according to the guidelines. There was, however, some opinion expressed quietly that man should have been created in the Committee's image.

And God caused a deep sleep to fall on the Committee... Author-Unknown

----

Letters From
Michigan's Upper Peninsula

As you know, there are a lot of Californians & Texans moving to Michigan's Upper Peninsula these days. Unlike the U.P. with its four seasons, California only has two; Hot, and hot as hell. The following excerpts are from the diary of someone who recently moved to Calumet, Michigan.

MyDiary

November 1
It started to snow this evening about 5:00 p.m., our first of the season. My wife and I took our cocktails and sat for hours by the window watching the huge, soft flakes drift down from the heavens. They say that no two snowflakes are the same! It was so beautiful.

We awoke to a big wonderful blanket of crystal-white snow covering our yard as far as the eye could see. Could there be a more wonderful place in the world? Moving here was the best idea I've ever had. I shoveled for the first time in over 30 years...and loved it, did both the driveway and sidewalk. Of course two minutes after I finished, the snowplow came by and covered it all up again with the compacted snow from the street. Oh well, I took it in stride and shoveled it all again.

November 7
The sun melted all our lovely snow. Such a disappointment. My neighbor tells me not to worry, we'll definitely have a white Christmas. No snow on Christmas would be awful! Our neighbor John says we'll have so much snow by the end of winter, I'll never want to see snow again. I don't think that's possible. John is such a nice man. I'm glad he's our neighbor.

November 10
Got another 8 inches of snow last night and the temperature dropped to 20 below zero. The cold makes everything sparkle so. Shoveled the driveway so I could get the car out, but before I could open the garage

door, the snowplow did his thing again. It worked out for the best, because the car wouldn't start anyway. I fixed myself a drink and laughed it off.

November 19

I sold the car and bought a 4 wheel drive truck. The wife wants a stove in case the electricity goes out. I think that's silly. We aren't living in Alaska after all. Fell on my ass on the ice in the driveway getting into it. My wife laughed for an hour, which I think was cruel. Still cold, below zero every morning, and the icy roads make for tough driving. I did however make it to the liquor store and bought enough booze to last the winter. The jerk in the snowplow came by while I was gone and covered the driveway again.

November 23

Happy friggin' holidays in the U.P. We're assured a white Christmas this year because 6 more inches of the "White Shit" fell today. Forget that crap about snowflakes all looking different. You've seen one, you've seen them all!!! Anyway, I took a couple of stiff belts out of the whiskey bottle and suited up to shovel the driveway. Boots, jump suit, heavy jacket, scarf, ear muffs, gloves, etc. Got in one shovelful and had to piss like a Russian race horse. Figured I'd risk blowing a kidney and finish the job. When I did, I ran for the house and just made it to the toilet. While I was standing relieving myself, I heard a now familiar sound. Yes, that cocksucker in the snowplow did it again. The only reason to get out was that the liquor cabinet was empty again!! I think the wife has been sipping a little behind my back. Selfish Bitch!

November 30

Still way below freezing. Roads are too icy to go anywhere. Electricity was off for 5 hours. Had to pile the blankets on to stay warm. No TV. Nothing to do but stare at the wife and try to irritate her. Guess we should've bought the wood stove, but won't admit it to HER! Man, I hate it when she's right. I can't believe that I'm freezing to death in my own living room.

December 4

Electricity is back on, but had another 14" of the damn stuff last night. More shoveling. Took all day. The friggin' snowplow came by twice. Tried to find a neighbor kid to shovel but they say they're too busy playing hockey. I think they're lying. Called the only hardware store around to see about purchasing a snow blower and they're out. Might get another shipment in May. I think they're lying. Bob says I have to shovel or the city will have it done and bill me. I think he's lying.

December 8

If I ever catch the son-of-a-bitch that drives that snowplow, I'll drag his bare ass through the white shit from here to the city limits. The temperature stays at zero or below all day. If this keeps up I'll be screwing with this white shit till August. Got to get to the liquor store before it closes. I caught the wife dead on her ass drunk on the bathroom floor yesterday. At least now I know where the booze is going.

December 10, 11, or 12

8 more inches. If it wasn't for going to the liquor store, I'd never get out. Must be cabin fever or I'm going snow-blind from the white shit all over my yard, but even that drunken slut I married is starting to look good. Doesn't matter, It's so cold I have to tie a string and tag on my dick just to find it every morning.

December 18

Toilet froze. If you go outside, don't eat the brown snow, ha ha! My neighbor John came by and told me I better get some of that white shit off my roof or it might cave in. He must think I'm stupid Screw it and the snowplow. Liquor store has started making deliveries to the front door. I ain't going out till this shit melts all the way.

December 22

John was right about a white Christmas because 13 more inches of the white crap fell today and it's so cold it probably won't melt until August. Broke the snow shovel, thought I was having a heart attack. Took me an hour to clear 2/3rds of the drive.

December 24
Roof caved in. Wife went home with her mother as predicted. Set fire to what was left of the house. No more shoveling.

December 25,
Newberry Mental Hospital

Merry Christmas my ass. My lawyer says I should be out in a year or two. All this could have been avoided if the snowplow driver hadn't come by asking for a donation for some charity. His doctor testified at my trial that there was no permanent damage to his rectum from my assault with the snow shovel handle. It was wrong, I know that now. The arson charge, too, could have been avoided.

I really feel bad about the guy who owns the liquor store. Ever since we left the neighborhood, the bank foreclosed on his new house and the Cadillac dealer repossessed his new car. Even the kid who used to deliver for him quit, claimed he wasn't making the $1500 a week like when we lived there.

End of Diary

Hot enough for you today?

As many already know, there are those who call themselves snowbirds, meaning that they have a Summer and Winter home. The Summer home is in the northern United States, and the Winter home in the Southern United States to avoid the unpleasant bitter cold of Winter. The following is a Diary of someone who moved from Michigan's Upper Peninsula to Texas, but I could well apply for California or Florida.

Dear Diary:

May 30th:

Just moved to Dallas...Now this is a city that knows how to live!! Beautiful sunny days and warm balmy evenings. What a place! Watched the sunset from a park lying on a blanket. It was beautiful. I've finally found my home. I love it here.

June 14th:

Really heating up. Got to 100 today. Not a problem. Live in an air-conditioned home, drive an air-conditioned car. What a pleasure to see the sun every day like this. I'm turning into a sun worshipper.

June 30th:

Had the backyard landscaped with western plants today. Lots of cactus and rocks. What a breeze to maintain. No more mowing lawn for me. Another scorcher today, but I love it here.

July 10th:

The temperature hasn't been below 100 all week. How do people get used to this kind of heat? At least it's kind of windy though. But getting used to the heat and humidity, just taking a bit longer than I expected.

July 15th:

Fell asleep by the pool. (Got 3rd degree burns over 60% of my body). Missed 3 days of work. What a dumb thing to do. I learned my lesson though. Got to respect the ol' sun in a climate like this.

July 20th:

I missed Morgan (our cat) sneaking into the car when I left this morning. By the time I got to the hot car for lunch, Morgan had died and swollen up to the size of a shopping bag and stank up the $2,000 leather upholstery. I told the kids that she ran away. The car now smells like Kibbles and shits. I learned my lesson though. No more pets in this heat.

July 25th:

The wind sucks. It feels like a giant freaking blow dryer!! And it's hot as hell. The home air-conditioner is on the fritz and the AC repairman charged $200 just to drive by and tell me he needed to order parts.

July 30th:

Been sleeping outside by the pool for 3 nights now. $1,500 in damn house payments and we can't even go inside. Why did I ever come here?

Aug. 4th:

It's 115 degrees. Finally got the air-conditioner fixed today. It cost $500 and gets the temperature down to 85, but this freaking humidity makes the house feel like it's about 95. Stupid repairman pissed in my pool. I hate this stupid city.

Aug. 8th:

If another wise ass cracks, "Hot enough for you today?", I'm going to strangle him. Damn heat. By the time I get to work the radiator is boiling over, my clothes are soaking wet, and I smell like baked cat!!

Aug. 9th:

Tried to run some errands after work. Wore shorts, and sat on the black leather seats in the ol' car. I thought my ass was on fire. I lost 2 layers of flesh and all the hair on the back of my legs and ass. Now my car smells like burnt hair, fried ass, and baked cat.

Aug. 10th:

The weather report might as well be a damn recording. Hot and sunny, Hot and sunny, Hot and sunny. It's been too hot to do shit for 2 damn months and the weatherman says it might really warm up next week. Doesn't it ever rain in this damn desert?? Water rationing will be next, so might $1700 worth of cactus just dry up and blow into the damn pool. Even the cactus can't live in this damn heat.

Aug. 14th:

Welcome to HELL!!! Temperature got to 115 today. Forgot to crack the window and blew the damn windshield out of the car. The installer came to fix it and said, "Hot enough for you today?" My wife had to spend the $1500 house payment to bail me out of jail. Freaking Texas. What kind of a sick demented idiot would want to live here??

Company Christmas Party

December 1 TO: ALL EMPLOYEES
I'm happy to inform you that the company Christmas Party will take place on December 23rd at Luigi's Open Pit Barbecue. There will be lots of spiked eggnog and a small band playing traditional carols...feel free to sing along. And please don't be surprised if our CEO shows up dressed as Santa Claus to light the Christmas tree! Exchange of gifts among employees can be done at that time; however, no gift should be over $10. Merry Christmas to you and your family. Patty Lewis Human Resources Director

December 2nd TO: ALL EMPLOYEES
In no way was yesterday's memo intended to exclude our Jewish employees. We recognize that Hanukkah is an important holiday that often coincides with Christmas (though unfortunately not this year). However, from now on we're calling it our "Holiday Party." The same policy applies to employees who are celebrating Kwanzaa at this time. There will be no Christmas tree and no Christmas carols sung.

Happy Holidays to you and your family. Patty Lewis Human Resources Director

December 3rd TO: ALL EMPLOYEES

Regarding the anonymous note I received from a member of Alcoholics anonymous requesting a non-drinking table, I'm happy to accommodate this request, but, don't forget, if I put a sign on the table that reads, "AA Only," you won't be anonymous anymore. In addition, forget about the gifts exchange-- no gifts will be allowed since the union members feel that $10 is too much money.

Patty Lewis Human Researchers Director

December 7th TO: ALL EMPLOYEES

I've arranged for members of Overeaters Anonymous to sit farthest from the dessert buffet and pregnant women closest to the restrooms. Gays are allowed to sit with each other. Lesbians do not have to sit with the gay men; each will have their table. Yes, there will be a flower arrangement for the gay men's table. Happy now?

Patty Lewis Human Racehorses Director

December 9th TO: ALL EMPLOYEES

People, people -- nothing sinister was intended by wanting our CEO to play Santa Claus! Even if the anagram of "Santa" does happen to be "Satan," there is no evil connotation to our own "little man in a red suit."

Patty Lewis Human Ratraces

December 10th TO: ALL EMPLOYEES

Vegetarians -- I've had it with you people!! We're going to hold this party at Luigi's Open Pit whether you like it or not, you can just sit at the table farthest from the "grill of death," as you put it, and you'll get salad bar only, including hydroponic tomatoes. But, you know, tomatoes have feelings, too. They scream when you slice them. I've heard them scream. I'm hearing them right now... Ha! I hope you all have a rotten holiday! Drive drunk and die, you hear me?

The Bitch from Hell

December 14th TO: ALL EMPLOYEES
I'm sure I speak for all of us in wishing Patty Lewis a speedy recovery from her stress-related illness. I'll continue to forward your cards to her at the sanitarium. In the meantime, management has decided to cancel our Holiday Party and give everyone the afternoon of the 23rd off with full pay.

Happy Holidays! Terri Bishop Acting Human Resources Director

Thinkers Anonymous:
It started out innocently enough. I began to think at parties now and then to loosen up. Inevitably though, one thought led to another, and soon I was more than just a social thinker. I began to think alone - "to relax" I told myself - but I knew it wasn't true. Thinking became more and more important to me, and finally I was thinking all the time.

I began to think on the job. I knew that thinking and employment don't mix, but I couldn't stop myself.
I began to avoid friends at lunchtime so I could read Thoreau and Kafka. I would return to the office dizzied and confused, asking, "What exactly are we doing here?"

Things weren't going so great at home either. One evening I had turned off the TV and asked my wife about the meaning of life. She spent that night at her mother's. I soon had a reputation as a heavy thinker. One day the boss called me in. He said, "I like you, and it hurts me to say this, but your thinking has become a real problem. If you don't stop thinking on the job, you'll have to find another job." This gave me a lot to think about.

I came home early after my conversation with the boss. "Honey", I confessed, "I've been thinking,

"I know you've been thinking," she said, "and I want a divorce." "But honey, surely it's not that serious." "It is serious," she said, lower lip aquiver. "You think as much as college professors, and college professors don't make any money, so if you keep on thinking we won't have any money!"

"That's a faulty syllogism," I said impatiently, and she began to cry. "I've had enough. I'm going to the library," I snarled as I stomped out the door. I headed for the library, in the mood for some Nietzsche. I roared into the parking lot and ran up to the big glass doors they didn't open. The library was closed.

As I sank to the ground clawing at the unfeeling glass, whimpering for Zarathustra, a poster caught my eye. "My friend, is heavy thinking ruining your life?" it asked. You probably recognize that line. It comes from the standard Thinkers Anonymous poster.

Which is why I am what I am today, a recovering thinker. I never miss a TA meeting. At each meeting we watch a non-educational video; last week it was "Porky's." Then we share experiences about how we avoided thinking since last meeting. I still have my job, and things are a lot better at home. Life just seemed easier, somehow, as soon as I stopped thinking.

Once upon a time many, many years ago....In the North Pole, Santa was very cross. It was Christmas Eve and NOTHING was going right. Mrs. Claus had burned all the cookies. The elves were complaining about not getting paid for the overtime they had while making the toys. The reindeer had been drinking all afternoon and were dead drunk. To make matters worse, they had taken the sleigh out for a spin earlier in the day and had crashed it into a tree.

Santa was furious. "I can't believe it! I've got to deliver millions of presents all over the world in just a few hours - all of my reindeer are drunk, the elves are on strike and I don't even have a Christmas tree! I sent that stupid Little Angel out HOURS ago to find a tree and he hasn't come back yet!

Just then, the Little Angel opened the front door and stepped in from the snowy night, dragging a Christmas tree. He says, "Yo, fat man! Where do you want me to stick the tree this year?" And thus the tradition of angels atop the Christmas trees came to pass........

Dear Santa...A Mother's Xmas Wishes

I've been a good Mom all year. I've fed, cleaned, and cuddled my two children on demand, visited the doctor's office more than my doctor, sold sixty-two cases of candy bars to raise money to plant a shade tree on the school playground and figured out how to attach nine patches onto my daughter's girl scout sash with staples and a glue gun. I was hoping you could spread my list out over several Christmases, since

I had to write this letter with my son's red crayon, on the back of a receipt in the laundry room between cycles, and who knows when I find any more free time in the next 18 years.

Here are my Christmas wishes: I'd like a pair of legs that don't ache after a day of chasing kids (in any color, except purple,) which I already have, and arms that don't flap in the breeze, but are still strong enough to carry a screaming toddler out of the candy aisle in the grocery store. I'd also like a waist line, since I lost mine somewhere in the seventh month of my last pregnancy.

If you're hauling big ticket items this year, I'd like a car with fingerprint resistant windows and a radio that only plays adult music, a television that doesn't broadcast any programs containing talking animals; and a refrigerator with a secret compartment behind the crisper where I can hide to talk on the phone.

On the practical side, I could use a talking daughter doll that says "Yes, Mommy" to boost my parental confidence, along with one potty-trained toddler, two kids who don't fight, and three pairs of jeans that will zip all the way up without the use of power tools. I could also use a recording of Tibetan monks chanting, "Don't eat in the living room" and 'Take your hands off your brother,' because my voice seems to be just out of my children's hearing range and can only be heard by the dog, and please don't forget the Playdoh Travel Pack, the stocking stuffer this year for mothers of preschoolers. It comes in three fluorescent colors and is guaranteed to crumble on any carpet making the In-laws' house seem just like mine.

If it's too late to find any of these products, I'd settle for enough time to brush my teeth and comb my hair in the same morning, or the luxury of eating food warmer than room temperature without it being served in a Styrofoam container. If you don't mind I could also use a few Christmas miracles to brighten the holiday season.

Would it be too much trouble to declare ketchup a vegetable? It will clear my conscience immensely. It would be helpful if you could coerce my children to help around the house without demanding payment as if they were the bosses of an organized crime family; or if my toddler didn't look so cute sneaking downstairs to eat contraband ice cream in his pajamas at midnight.

Well, Santa, the buzzer on the dryer is ringing and my son saw my feet under the laundry room door. I think he wants his crayon back. Have a safe trip and remember to leave your wet boots by the chimney and come in and dry off by the fire so you don't catch cold. Help yourself to cookies on the table, but don't eat too many or leave crumbs on the carpet.

Yours Always...Mom. PS One more thing...you can cancel all my requests if you can keep my children young enough to believe in you.

SANTA CLAUS IS A WOMAN

I hate to be the one to defy sacred myth, but I believe he's a she. Think about it. Christmas is a big, organized, warm, fuzzy, nurturing, social deal, and I have a tough time believing a guy could possibly pull it all off!

For starters, the vast majority of men don't even think about selecting gifts until Christmas Eve. Once at the mall, they always seem surprised to find only Ronco products, socket wrench sets, and mood rings left on the shelves.

On this count alone, I'm convinced Santa is a woman. Surely, if he were a man, everyone in the universe would wake up Christmas morning to find a rotating musical Chia Pet under the tree, still in the bag.

Another problem for a he-Santa would be getting there. First of all, there would be no reindeer because they would all be dead, gutted and strapped on to the rear bumper of the sleigh amid wide-eyed, desperate claims that buck season had been extended. Blitzen's rack would already be on the way to the taxidermist.

Even if the male Santa DID have reindeer, he'd still have transportation problems because he would inevitably get lost up there in the snow and clouds and then refuse to stop and ask for directions. Other reasons why Santa can't possibly be a man:

-Men can't pack a bag.
-Men would rather be dead than caught wearing red velvet.
-Men would feel their masculinity is threatened...having to be seen with all those elves.
-Men don't answer their mail.
-Men would refuse to allow their physique to be described, even in jest, as anything remotely resembling a "bowl full of jelly."

-Men aren't interested in stockings unless somebody's wearing them.
-Having to do the Ho Ho Ho thing would seriously inhibit their ability to pick up women.

Finally, being responsible for Christmas would require a commitment.

I can buy the fact that other mythical holiday characters are men:

Father Time shows up once a year unshaven and looking ominous. Definite guy.

Cupid flies around carrying weapons.

Uncle Sam is a politician who likes to point fingers.

Any one of these individuals could pass the testosterone screening test. But not St. Nick.

Letters from Miss Edith Smith
to
John

December 14

Dearest John,

How is everything? I just wanted to take the time to tell you that I went to the door today and the Postman delivered a partridge in a pear tree, what a thoughtful gift. I really couldn't have been more surprised. Thank you so much.

With Deepest Love & Devotion,

Edith

December 15

Dearest John,

I just can't get over this! Today the Postman brought your very sweet gift. Just imagine two turtle doves. I'm just delighted about your very thoughtful gift. They are just adorable.

All My Love,

Edith

December 16

Dearest John,

Oh! Aren't you the extravagant one. Now I really must protest. I don't deserve such generosity, three French Hens. They are just darling, but I must insist, you've been too kind.

Love,

Edith

December 17

Dear John,

Today the postman delivered four calling birds. Now really, they are beautiful, but don't you think enough is enough? You're being just a little too romantic, don't you think?

Affectionately,

Edith

December 18

Dearest John,

What a surprise! Today the Postman delivered five golden rings, one for every finger. You are just impossible, but I love it. Frankly, all those birds squawking were beginning to get on my nerves.

All My Love,

Edith

December 19

Dear John,

When I opened the door there were actually six geese a laying on my front porch. So you're back to the birds again--aye? Those geese are huge. Where will I ever keep them? The neighbors are complaining and I can't sleep through all the racket. Please Stop!

Cordially,

Edith

December 20

John,

What's with you and those friggin' birds? Seven swans a swimming? What kind of friggin' joke is this? There's bird shit all over the house and they never stop with the racket. I can't sleep at night and I'm such a nervous wreck. It's not funny, so stop with those friggin' birds.

Sincerely,

Edith

December 21

OK Buster,

I think I prefer the birds. What the hell am I going to do with eight maids a milking? It's not enough with all those birds and eight maids a milking, but they had to bring their stinking cows. There is shit all over the lawn and I can't move in my own house. Just lay off me, smartass...

Edith

December 22

Hey Shithead,

What are you, some kind of sadist? Now there's nine pipers playing. They just don't know when to quit. They've never stopped chasing those maids since they got here yesterday morning. The cows are getting upset and they're stepping all over those screeching birds. What am I going to do? The neighbors have started a petition to evict me.

You'll get yours,

Edith

December 23

You Rotten Prick!

Now there's ten ladies dancing. I don't know why I call those sluts ladies. They've been balling those pipers all night long. Now the cows can't sleep and they've got the runs. My living room is a river of shit and the building commissioner has subpoenaed me to give because why the building shouldn't be condemned.

I'm sicking the police on you!

One who means it!

December 24

Listen Dickhead!

What's with the eleven lords a leaping on those maids and ladies? Some of those broads will never walk again. Those pipers ran through the maids and have been committing sodomy with the cows. All twenty-three birds are dead, they've been trampled to death in the orgy. I hope you're satisfied, you rotten son-of-a-bitch!

Your Sworn Enemy,

Edith

December 25
Law Offices

Dewey, Cheatum & Howe

Colorado Springs, CO 80920

Dear Sir:

As attorneys for Miss Edith Smith, we acknowledge your latest gift of twelve fiddlers fiddling which you have seen fit to inflict on our client. The destruction, of course, was total. All correspondence should come to our attention. If you should attempt to reach Miss Smith at Happy Valley Sanitarium, the attendants have instructions to shoot you on sight. A restraining order has been issued prohibiting your visitation and please find attached a warrant for your arrest.

Cordially,

Dewey, Cheatum & Howe

Southern Christmas:

A new contract for Santa has finally been negotiated ...Please read the following carefully.......

I regret to inform you that, effective immediately, I will no longer be able to serve Southern United States on Christmas Eve. Due to the overwhelming current population of the earth, my contract was renegotiated by North American Fairies and Elves Local 209. I now serve only certain areas of Ohio, Indiana, Illinois, Wisconsin and Michigan. As part of the new and better contract I also get longer breaks for milk and cookies so keep that in mind. However, I'm certain that your children will be in good hands with your local replacement who happens to be my third cousin, Bubba Claus. His side of the family is from the South Pole. He shares my goal of delivering toys to all the good boys and girls; however, there are a few differences between us.

Differences such as:

1. There is no danger of a Grinch stealing your presents from Bubba Claus. He has a gun rack on his sleigh and a bumper sticker that reads: "These toys insured by Smith and Wesson."

2. Instead of milk and cookies, Bubba Claus prefers that children leave an RC cola and pork rinds [or a moon pie] on the fireplace And Bubba doesn't smoke a pipe. He dips a little snuff though, so please have an empty spit can handy.

3. Bubba Claus' sleigh is pulled by floppy-eared, flyin' coon dogs instead of reindeer. I made the mistake of loaning him a couple of my reindeer one time, and Blitzen's head now overlooks Bubba's fireplace.

4. You won't hear "On Comet, on Cupid, on Donner and Blitzen ..." when Bubba Claus arrives. Instead, you'll hear, "On Earnhardt, on Wallace, on Martin and Labonte. On Rudd, on Jarrett, on Elliott and Petty."

5. "Ho, ho, ho!" has been replaced by "Yee Haw!" And you also are likely to hear Bubba's elves respond, "I her'd dat!"

6. As required by Southern highway laws, Bubba Claus' sleigh does have a Yosemite Sam safety triangle on the back with the words "Back off". The last I heard it also had other decorations on the sleigh back as well. One is a Ford or Chevy logo with lights that race through the letters and the other is a caricature of me (Santa Claus) going weewee on the Tooth Fairy.

7. The usual Christmas movie classics such as "Miracle on 34th Street" and "It's a Wonderful Life" will not be shown in your negotiated viewing area. Instead, you'll see "Boss Hogg Saves Christmas" and "Smokey and the Bandit IV" featuring Burt Reynolds as Bubba Claus and dozens of state patrol cars crashing into each other.

8. Bubba Claus doesn't wear a belt. If I were you, I'd make sure you, the wife, and the kids turn the other way when he bends over to put presents under the tree.

9. And finally, lovely Christmas songs have been sung about me like "Rudolph The Red-nosed Reindeer" and Bing Crosby's "Santa Claus Is Coming to Town." This year songs about Bubba Claus will be played on all the AM radio stations in the South. Those song title Cledus T. Judd's "All I Want for Christmas Is My Woman and a Six Pack", and Hank Williams Jr.'s "If You Don't Like Bubba Claus, You can Shove It."

Sincerely Yours,
Santa Claus
(member of North American Fairies and Elves Local 209)

Does Santa Exist?

An Engineer's Perspective

1. There are approximately two billion children (persons under 18) in the world. However, since Santa does not visit children of Muslim, Hindu, Jewish, or Buddhist religions, this reduces the workload for Christmas night to 15% of the total, or 378 million according to the Population Reference Bureau). At an average (census) rate of 3.5 children per household, that comes to 108 million homes, presuming that there is at least one good child in each.

2. Santa has about 31 hours of Christmas to work with, thanks to the different time zones and the rotation of the earth, assuming he travels east to west (which seems logical). This works out to 967.7 visits per second. This is to say that for each Christian household with a good child, Santa has around 1/1,000th of a second to park the sleigh, hop out, jump down the chimney, fill the stockings, distribute the remaining presents under the tree, eat whatever snacks have been left for him, get back up the chimney, jump into the sleigh and get on to the next house. Assuming that each of these 108 million stops is evenly distributed around the earth (which, of course, we know to be false, but will accept for the purposes of our calculations), we are now talking about 0.78 miles per household; a total trip of 75.5 million miles, not counting bathroom stops or breaks. This means Santa's sleigh is moving at 650 miles per second --- 3,000 times the speed of sound. For purposes of comparison, the fastest man made vehicle, the Ulysses space probe, moves at a poky 27.4 miles per second, and a conventional reindeer can run (at best) 15 miles per hour.

3. The payload of the sleigh adds another interesting element. Assuming that each child gets nothing more than a medium sized logo set (two pounds), the sleigh is carrying over 500 thousand tons, not counting Santa himself. On land, a conventional reindeer can pull no more than 300 pounds. Even granting that the "flying" reindeer could pull ten times the normal amount, the job can't be done with eight or even nine of them. Santa would need 360,000 of them. This increases the payload, not counting the weight of the sleigh, another 54,000 tons, or roughly seven times the weight of the Queen Elizabeth (the ship, not the monarch).

4. 600,000 tons traveling at 650 miles per second creates enormous air resistance. This would heat up the reindeer in the same fashion as a spacecraft re-entering the earth's atmosphere. The lead pair of reindeer would absorb 14.3 quintillion joules of energy per second each. In short, they would burst into flames almost instantaneously, exposing the reindeer behind them and creating deafening sonic booms in their wake. The reindeer team would be vaporized within 4.26 thousandths of a second, or right about the time Santa reached the fifth house on his trip. Not that it matters, however, since Santa, as a result of accelerating from a dead stop to 650 m.p.s. in .001 seconds, would be subjected to centrifugal forces of 17,500 g's. A 250 pound Santa (which seems ludicrously slim) would be pinned to the back of the sleigh by 4,315,015 pounds of force, instantly crushing his bones and organs and reducing him to a quivering blob of pink goo.

5. Therefore, if Santa did exist, he's dead now.

Contributed by Spy Magazine

Does Santa Exist?

A Rebuttal

1. Santa does not have special reindeer, but rather enables ordinary reindeer to fly by special deer feed. (Don't ask Santa for the formula; I did once and he left me off the list for years - see #2)

2. With regard to the issue of how many homes Santa must visit: Not every one of the homes has even a single child that can qualify as good. Santa has very high standards, especially with regard to greedy letters most kids send. Better luck next year.

3. With regard to speed, if you ask any good physicist, she will tell you that time slows down as you move close to the speed of light. Since Santa's sleigh is powered by the Christmas Star, it travels at the speed of light. He actually arrives at the next location BEFORE he left the last one (traveling East, remember?). With regard to the time it takes to set up the presents and fill the stockings, Santa is non-union, so it doesn't take him as long as you would expect. Side note: all that high-speed travel reverses the aging process. That is why Santa comes just once a year. If he did it twice a year he would have been a baby again, around 1900.

4. Santa's bag of toys is actually a portal through the time/space continuum, like a wormhole. It connects directly to the North Pole warehouse. (Like beaming the stuff directly like in Star Trek).

5. With regard to the friction, Santa's entire sleigh is designed to overt the heat of the friction to run Santa's bag of toys (see #4). The sonic booms are canceled out by the frequency of the special sleigh bells.

In conclusion, Santa does exist. All that running around does require a lot of energy, though; so please remember to leave him some milk and cookies (especially chocolate chip). And if you see him, tell him I don't want the reindeer formula anymore . . . and the folks over at SPY magazine do.

"T'WAS THE NIGHT BEFORE CHRISTMAS

T'was the night before Christmas
And all through the house
Everybody felt shitty;
Yes, even the mouse.

Mom on the toilet,
Dad smoking grass;
I had just settled down
For a nice piece of ass.
When up on the roof-top
I heard such a clatter
I ran up the steps
To see just what was the matter.

I looked out the window
And saw some old prick
I knew in an instant
It must be Saint Nick.

He came down the chimney
Like a bat out of hell,
I knew in a second
The sucker had fell.

He filled all the stockings
Full of whiskey and beer
And a big rubber dick
For my brother, the _____.

He rose up the chimney
With a thunderous fart
The son-of-a-bitch
Blew my chimney apart.

And I heard him s
As he rode out of sight
Piss on you-all
It's been one hell of a night.

Author: Unknown - thank goodness.

Santa Is Quitting His Job
Received via Email, no authorship given.

T'was the night before Christmas--Old Santa was pissed.
He cussed out the elves and threw down his list.
Miserable little brats, ungrateful little jerks
I have a good mind to scrap the whole works!

I've busted my ass for damn near a year,
Instead of "Thanks Santa"--what do I hear?
The old lady bitches cause I work late at night
The elves want more money--The reindeer all fight.

Rudolph got drunk and goosed all the maids
Donner is pregnant and Vixen has AIDS
And just when I thought that things would get better
Those assholes from the IRS sent me a letter,

They say I owe taxes--if that ain't damn funny
Who the hell ever sent Santa Claus any money?
And the kids these days--they all are the pits
They want the impossible--Those mean little shits

I spent a whole year making wagons and sleds
Assembling dolls...Their arms, legs and heads
I made a ton of Yo-Yo's--NO request for them,
They want computers and robot; they think I'm IBM!

Flying through the air; and dodging the trees
Falling down chimneys and skinning my knees
I'm quitting this job; there's just no enjoyment
I'll sit on my fat ass and draw unemployment.

There's no Christmas this year; now you know the reason,
I found me a blonde. I'm going SOUTH for the season

THE JOY OF COOKING FOR CHRISTMAS

T'was the night before Christmas and all through the kitchen;
I was cooking and baking and moanin and bitchin.
I've been here for hours, I can't stop to rest.
This rooms a disaster, just look at this mess!

Tomorrow I've got thirty people to feed.
They expect all the trimmings. Who cares what I need!
My feet are both blistered, I've got cramps in my legs.
The cat just knocked over a bowl full of eggs.

There's a knock at the door and the telephones ringing;
frosting drips on the counter as the microwaves dinging.
Two pies in the oven, desserts almost done;
my cookbook is soiled with butter and crumbs.
I've had all I can stand, I can't take anymore;

Then in walks my husband, spilling rum on the floor.
He weaves and he wobbles, his balance unsteady;
Then grins as he chuckles "The eggnog is ready!"
He looks all around and with total regret,
ays "What's taking so long....aren't you through in here yet ??"

As quick as a flash I reach for a knife;
He loses an earlobe; I wanted his life!
He flees from the room in terror and pain
and screams "MY GOD WOMAN, YOU'RE GOING INSANE!!"

Now what was I doing, and what is that smell?
Oh shit it's the pies!! They're burned all to hell!!
I hate to admit when I make a mistake,
but I put them on BROIL instead of on BAKE.
What else can go wrong?? Is there still more ahead??
If this is good living, I'd rather be dead.
Lord, don't get me wrong, I love holidays;

It just leaves me exhausted, all shaky and dazed.
But I promise you one thing, If I live till next year,
You won't find me pulling my hair out in here.
I'll hire a maid, a cook, and a waiter;
and if that doesn't work,
I'LL HAVE IT ALL CATERED!!!

Subject: Whiskey

I had eighteen bottles of whiskey in my cellar and was told by my sister to empty the contents of each and every bottle down the sink, or else...

I said I would and proceeded with the unpleasant task. I withdrew the cork from the first bottle and poured the contents down the sink, with the exception of one glass, which I drank. I then withdrew the cork from the second bottle and did likewise with it, with the exception of one glass, which I drank. I then withdrew the cork from the third bottle and poured the whiskey in the sink which I drank.

I pulled the cork from the fourth bottles down the sink and

poured the bottle down the glass, which I drank. I pulled the bottle from the cork of the next and drank one sink out of it, and threw the rest down the glass. I pulled the sink out of the next glass and poured the cork down the bottle. Then I corked the sink with glass, bottled the drink and drank the pour. When I had everything emptied, I steadied the house with one hand, counted the glasses, corks, bottles, and sinks with the other, which were twenty-nine, and as the houses came by I counted them again, and finally I had all the houses in one bottle, which I drank. I'm not under the affluence of alcohol as some tinkle peep I am. I'm not half as thunk as you might drink either. I fool so feelish I don't know who is me, and the drunker I stand here, the longer I get.

"THE BEST RUM CAKE EVER"

If the hustle and bustle of Christmas is about to get you down, try the following recipe. It was sent to me and is called: The Best Rum Cake Ever; One or two quarts rum, one cup butter, one teaspoon sugar, two large eggs, one cup dried fruit, one teaspoon soda, lemon juice, brown sugar, nuts, and baking powder.

Before you start, sample the rum to check for quality. (Good, isn't it?) Now go ahead. Select a large mixing bowl, measuring cup, etc. Check the rum again. It must be just right. To be sure rum is of the highest quality, pour one level cup of rum into a glass and drink it as fast as you can. Repeat as many times as you need.

With an electric mixer, beat one cup butter in a large fluffy bowl. Add one seaspoon of thugar and beat again. Meanwhile, make sure that the rum is of the finest quality - try another cup. Open second quart if necessary. Add two arge leggs, two cups fried druit and beat till high. If druit gets stuck in beaters, just pry it loose with a drewscriver and add a wittle bit more run. Sample run again checking for tonscisiticity.

Next sift three cups pepper or salt (it really doesn't matter which at this point). Sample the rum again. Sift 1/2 pint of lemon juice.

Fold in chipped butter and strained nuts. Add one babblespoon of brown thugar, or whatever color you can find. Wix mel. Grease oven and turn cake pan to 350 gredees. Now pour the whole mess into the coven and ake. Check the rum again and go to bed.

Mewwy Cwistmas

TROJAN CONDOM COMPANY

6969 Slippery Root Drive
Drop Trouser, North Carolina 27061-1812

We regret to inform you that we have rejected your recent application to model and represent our product, Trojan Condoms.

Although your general physical appearance is not displeasing, our Board of Directors feels that your wearing of our product does not portray a positive, romantic image for our line. A loose, baggy, and wrinkled condom is NOT considered romantic. We did admire your efforts to firm it up by using PoliGrip, but even then it slipped off before we could get the photographs taken. We would like to note, however, that we have never seen a penis that looked like a bicycle grip until now.

We appreciate your interest and thank you for your time. We will retain your application for future consideration, if by chance we decide that there is a market for Micro-Mini Condoms.

We send greetings and our deepest sympathy to any "partner" you may have in your life.

Yours very truly,

TROJAN CONDOM COMPANY

Burly Dick
President

PS: Remember our slogans:

> * *"Cover your stump before you hump!"*
> * *"Don't be silly, protect your willy!"*
> * *"Before you attack her, wrap your whacker!"*
> * *"If you're not going to sack it, go home and whack it!"*

NTERNAL REVENUE SERVICE
SUBJECT: TAX INCREASE
TO: ALL MALE TAXPAYERS

Dear Sir:

The Internal Revenue Service has taxed virtually everything. The only thing that we have not taxed is your pecker. This is due to the fact that 40% of the time it is hanging around unemployed, 30% of the time it is pissed off, 20% of the time it is hard up and the 10% of the time that it is employed it is operating in the hole. Furthermore, it has two dependents and both of them are nuts.

However, after April the 15th, your pecker will be taxed according to its size. Please refer to the Federal Pecker Checker Scale below. Determine your category and insert the additional tax under "Other Taxes," p.2, part V, line 69 on your standard income tax return.

Federal Pecker Checker Scale

*	10-12 inches - Luxury Tax	$50.00
*	8-10 inches - Pole Tax	$25.00
*	6-8 inches - Privilege Tax	$15.00
*	4-6 inches - Nuisance Tax	$5.00

Anything over 12 inches will be penalized for Capital Gains. If you are under four inches you may be eligible for a refund. Please do not apply for an extension.

Internal Revenue Service

Reuben J. Cutyourpeckeroff
Director

H&R Block rep's Note: Sometimes a story comes to our attention that needs no polishing or enhancement to make it a good Block tax story. This is one of those. It is a real letter submitted to the IRS in the midst of last year's weird and bizarre denial of dependents, exemptions, and credits. We believe the letter speaks for itself.

Dear Sirs:

I am responding to your letter denying the deduction for two of the three dependents I claimed on my 2019 Federal Tax return. Thank you. I have questioned whether these are my children or not for years. They are evil and expensive. It's only fair that since they are minors and not my responsibility that the government (who evidently is taxing me more to care for these waifs) knows something about them and what to expect over the next year. You may apply next year to reassign them to me and reinstate the deduction. This year they are yours!

The oldest, Kristen, is now 17. She is brilliant. Ask her! I suggest you put her to work in your office where she can answer people's questions about their returns. While she has no formal training, it has not seemed to hamper her knowledge of any other subject you can name. Taxes should be a breeze; Next year she is going to college. I think it's wonderful that you will now be responsible for that little expense. While you mull that over keep in mind that she has a truck. It doesn't run at the moment, so you have the immediate decision of appropriating some Department of Defense funds to fix the vehicle or getting up early to drive her to school.

Kristen also has a boyfriend. Oh joy. While she possesses all of the wisdom of the universe, her alleged mother and I have felt it best to occasionally remind her of the virtues of abstinence, and in the face of overwhelming passion and safe sex, this is always uncomfortable and I am quite relieved you will be handling this in the future. May I suggest that you reinstate Lauren Asato, who has a rather good handle on the problem?

Patrick is 14. I've had my suspicions about this one. His eyes are a little close together for normal people. He may be a tax examiner himself one day if you do not incarcerate him first. In February I was awakened at three in the morning by a police officer who was bringing Pat home. He and his friends T-pea houses as an occupation. In the future would you like him delivered to the local IRS office or to Ogden, UT?

Kids at 14 will do almost anything on a dare. His hair is purple. Permanent dye, temporary dye; what's the big deal? Learn to deal with it. You will have plenty of time as he is sitting out a few days from school after instigating a food fight. I'll take care of filing your phone number with the vice principal. Oh yes, he and all his friends have raging hormones.

This is the house of testosterone and it will be much more peaceful when he lives in your home. DO NOT leave any of them unsupervised with girls, explosives, inflammables, inflatable vehicles, or telephones. (I am sure that you will find telephones a source of unimaginable amusement and be sure to lock out the 900 and 976 numbers!)

Heather is an alien. She slid through a time warp and appeared quite by magic one year. I'm sure this one is yours. She is 10 going on 21. She came from a bad trip in the sixties. She wears tie-dyed clothes, beads, sandals, and her hair looks like Tiny Tim's.

Fortunately, you will be raising my taxes to help offset the pinch of her remedial reading courses. "Hooked on Phonics," is expensive so the schools dropped it. Good news! You can buy it yourself for half the amount of the deduction that you are denying! It's quite obvious that we were terrible parents (ask the other two) so they have helped raise this one to a new level of terror. She cannot speak English. Most people under twenty understand the curious patois she fashioned out of valley girls/boys in the hood/reggae/yuppie/ political doublespeak, I don't! The school sends her to a speech pathologist who has been rolling her roll R's. It added a refreshing Mexican/Irish touch to her voice. She wears hats backwards, pants baggy and wants one of her ears pierced four more times. There is a fascination with tattoos that worries me, but I am sure that you can handle it. Bring a truck when you come to get her, as she sort of "nests" in her room, and I think that it would be easier to move the entire thing than find out what it is really made of.

You denied two of the three exemptions so it is only fair you get to pick which two you will take. I prefer that you take the youngest, I will still go bankrupt with Kristen's college but then I am free!

If you take the two oldest then I still have time for counseling before Heather becomes a teenager. If you take the two girls then I won't feel so bad about putting Patrick in a military academy.

Please let me know of your decision as soon as possible as I have already increased the withholding on my W-4 to cover the $395 in additional tax and to make a down payment on an airplane.

Yours Truly,

Bob

Note: The taxpayer in question added this caveat at a later date; "Rats, they sent me the refund and allowed the deductions."

Dear IRS,

Enclosed is my 2019 tax return & payment. Please take note of the attached article from USA Today newspaper. In the article, you will see that the Pentagon is paying $171.50 for hammers and NASA has paid $600.00 for a toilet seat.

Please find enclosed four toilet seats (value $2400) and six hammers (value $1029). This brings my total payment to $3429.00. Please note the overpayment of $22.00 and apply it to the "Presidential Election Fund," as noted on my return. Might I suggest you send the fund a 1.5 inch screw?" (See attached article...HUD paid $22.00 for a 1.5 inch Phillips head screw.)

It has been a pleasure to pay my tax bill this year, and I look forward to paying it again next year.

Sincerely,

A satisfied taxpayer

When NASA first started sending up astronauts, they quickly discovered that ballpoint pens would not work in zero gravity. To combat the problem, NASA scientists spent a decade and $12 billion to develop a pen that writes in zero gravity, upside down, under water, on almost any surface including glass and at temperatures ranging from below freezing to 300°C. The Russians used a pencil.

The fire at Los Alamos has one significant consequence. A classified research paper was recovered from a bunker whose security systems were mostly destroyed by the fire. This document was made public the week following the fire. Actually it reveals nothing that we didn't already suspect. But it does show that the government has apparently known for some time that besides arsenic, lead, mercury, radon, strontium and plutonium, a new extremely deadly and pervasive element has been created. Investigators at a lab have created the heaviest element known to science.

This startling new discovery has been tentatively named Govern-mentium (Gv), but kept top secret. This new element has no protons or electrons, thus having an atomic number of 0. It does, however, have 1 neutron, 125 deputy neutrons, 75 supervisory neutrons, and 111 team leader neutrons, giving it an astounding atomic mass of 312. These 312 particles are held together by force-mediating particles called morons, which are in turn surrounded by vast quantities of lepton-like particles called peons.

Since it has no electrons, Governmentium is inert. However, once created it tends to be ubiquitous and can be detected as it impedes every reaction with which it comes into contact. According to its creators/discoverers, a minute amount of Governmentium causes one reaction to take over six days to complete when it would normally take less than a second. While Governmentium has a normal half-life of approximately four years; it does not decay but instead undergoes a spontaneous reorganization in which a portion of the deputy neutrons, supervisory neutrons, and team leader neutrons exchange places.

In fact, a Governmentium sample's mass will actually increase over time, since, with each reorganization some of the morons inevitably become neutrons forming new isotopes. This characteristic of moron promotion leads some scientists to speculate that Governmentium is formed whenever morons reach a certain quantity in concentration. This hypothetical quantity is referred to as the "Critical Morass".

Further information will be released at a specific time and place yet to be determined. "The place has been determined, but the exact time cannot be determined with certainty, for reasons that the knowledgeable reader will doubtless understand."

Once upon a time the government had a huge, abandoned scrap yard in the middle of the desert. A congressman discovered its existence, and worried that someone may steal from it at night. So they created a Night Watchman position and hired a man for the job.

Then Congress asked, "How can the watchman do his job without proper instruction?" So they created a Planning Department and hired two more people: a Documentation Specialist to write the instructions, and a trainer to teach the Night Watchman how to watch.

Then Congress said, "How will we know the Night Watchman and the Documentation Specialist are doing their tasks correctly?" So they created a Quality Control Department and hired two more people: one to do efficiency studies and one to write reports.

Then Congress said, "How are these people going to get paid?" So they created positions for an accountant, a Payroll Officer, and a Manager to keep track of everyone's time, and hired three more people.

Then Congress said, "Who's going to be accountable for all of these people?" So they created an Administrative Section and hired three more people: an

Administrative Officer, an Assistant Administrative Officer, and a Legal Secretary.

Then Congress said, "We have had this facility in operation for one year, and we are $22,000 over budget! We must cut back our overall costs!" So they laid off the Night Watchman.

Bill Clinton Statue Committee
100 Pennsylvania Avenue
Washington DC 20200-0001

Dear Tax Payer,

The Bill Clinton Statue Committee is trying to raise $5 million dollars to place the Bill Clinton Statue in the Hall of Fame in Washington DC. The committee was in a quandary, however, where to place the statue. It wasn't wise to place it beside the statue of George Washington, who never told a lie, or beside the statue of Jesse Jackson, who never told the truth, since Bill Clinton could never tell the difference.

After much debate they decided to place it beside the statue of Christopher Columbus, the greatest Democrat of us all. He left not knowing where he was going, didn't know where he was when he got there, left not knowing where he had been, and did it all on borrowed money.

Five thousand years ago, Moses told the children of Israel, "Pick up your shovels, mount your asses and camels and I will lead you to the promised land." Theodore Roosevelt said, "Put down your shovels, sit on your asses, light up a camel, this is the promised land. Bill Clinton is going to steal your shovels, kick your asses, tax your camels, and mortgage the promised land. If you have any money left over after paying taxes, the committee will expect a generous contribution to this worthwhile cause.

Sincerely,

From your friends in high places,

PS: It has been said that they are thinking of changing the party emblem from a donkey to a condom because it is virtually inflation proof, protects a bunch of pricks, halts production, and gives you a false sense of security while being screwed!

WHY I FIRED MY SECRETARY

When I awoke this morning, I was aware it wasn't an ordinary day. I felt an inner sense that made me want to close my eyes and go back to sleep. Then I remembered it was my birthday and at my age who needs another one of those.

I arose, showered, dressed and descended the stairs, bracing myself for the usual chorus of, "Happy Birthday" from the kids but there was none. Not even a cheerful, "Happy Birthday, Dear" from my wife. Instead of being grateful that so far the world had allowed me to ignore it, I felt even a deeper gloom.

As I entered my office my lovely blonde secretary greeted me with nothing more than, "Good morning Mr. Smith." Then at 11:30 it happened. My secretary came in all smiles and said, "It's such a beautiful day, I've decided to take you to a darling little place for lunch to celebrate your birthday."

We arrived, had a few drinks and a wonderful lunch. On the way back to the office she said, "Now we'll stop by my apartment where it is quiet and we will have more privacy." When we arrived, she mixed me a drink and then excused herself to change into something more comfortable. "Wow, I thought, this is a good world after all."

In just a few minutes she called out and said, "Are you ready for your little surprise?" I said, 'Sure!' Then her bedroom door opened and there she stood holding a huge birthday cake aglow with candles. There also stood my wife and kids and I stood there with nothing on but my socks.

Just because

I'm a Democrat

And you're a

Republican

We can Still be friends.

I'll hug your elephant

And you can kiss my

Ass.

VIAGRA DIARY...HER VERSON – Received via email, no authorship given.

Day 1 - Just celebrated our 25th wedding anniversary with not much to celebrate. When it came time to re-enact our wedding night, he locked himself in the bathroom and cried.

Day 2 - Today, he says he has a big secret to tell me. He's impotent, he says, and he wants me to be the first to know. Why doesn't he tell me something I don't know!! I mean, gimme a break! He's been dysfunctional for so long that he even walks with a limp!

Day 3 - This marriage is in trouble. A woman has needs! Yesterday, I saw a picture of the Washington Monument and burst into tears!

Day 4 - A miracle has happened! There's a new drug on the market that will fix his "problem." It's called Viagra. I told him that if he takes Viagra, things will be just like they were on our wedding night. He said, "This time, I'd rather not have your mother join us." I think this will work. I replaced his Prozac with the Viagra, hoping to lift something other than his mood.

Day 5 - Oh Happy Day! I feel like a new woman!!

Day 6 - Again! and Again! and Again!!! Whew, you sure can catch up on that in a big hurry!

Day 7 - This Viagra thing has gone to his head, no pun intended! Yesterday at Burger King the girl asked me if I'd like a Whopper and he thought they were talking about him. Get over yourself! Not everything is about you! But, I have to admit.....

Day 8 - I think he took too many over the weekend. Yesterday, instead of mowing the lawn, he was using his new friend as a weed whacker....

Day 10 - Okay, I admit it. I'm hiding. I mean, a girl can only take so much. And to make matters worse, he's washing the Viagra down with hard cider! The photo of Janet Reno isn't working - in fact, it may be making it worse. The picture of Hillary didn't help either! What am i gonna do? I feel tacky all over....

Day 11 - The side effects are starting to get to him. Everything is turning blue. The other day, we were watching Kenneth Branaugh in Hamlet and he thought it was "The Smurfs Do Denmark". Even my armpits hurt. He's a nasty man.

Day 12 - OK, I'm basically being drilled to death. It's like going out with a Black & Decker power tool. I woke up this morning feeling like I'd been hot-glued to the bed.

Day 13 - I wish he was gay. I bought 400 Liza Minelli albums and I keep saying, "Fabulous," and still he keeps coming after me! Even yawning has become dangerous...

Day 14 - Now I know how Saddam Hussein's wife feels. Every time I shut my eyes, there's a sneak attack! It's like going to bed with a Scud missile. Let's hope he's not like Ex-President Bush and takes 100 days to pullout. I can hardly walk and if he tries that "Oops, sorry" butt thing again, I'm gonna kill him.

Day 15 - I've done everything to turn him off. Nothing is working. I even started dressing like a nun. Now he tells me "Sister Wendy" makes "Father Woody" want to bark like a dog. Help me, please!!

Day 16 - The cats are afraid of him and the neighbors no longer come over. Last night I told him to screw himself........he did. I think I will have to kill him, then he'll go out the way he wants to ....stiff! With my luck, I won't be able to close the casket.

Received on Internet; No authorship given.

The following was written by State Representative Mitchell Kaye from Georgia.

"We, the sensible people of the United States, in an attempt to help everyone get along, restore some semblance of justice, avoid any more riots, keep our nation safe, promote positive behavior, and secure the blessings of debt free liberty to ourselves and our great-great-great-grandchildren, hereby try one more time to ordain and establish some common sense guidelines for the terminally whiny, guilt ridden, delusional, and other liberal, bed wetters. We hold these truths to be self-evident: that a whole lot of people are confused by the Bill of Rights and are so dim that they require a Bill of No Rights.

ARTICLE I: You do not have the right to a new car, big screen TV or any other form of wealth. More power to you if you can legally acquire them, but no one is guaranteeing anything.

ARTICLE II: You do not have the right to never be offended. This country is based on freedom, and that means freedom for everyone - not just you! You may leave the room, turn the channel, express a different opinion, etc., but the world is full of idiots, and probably always will be.

ARTICLE III: You do not have the right to be free from harm. If you stick a screwdriver in your eye, learn to be more careful, do not expect the tool manufacturer to make you and all your relatives independently wealthy.

ARTICLE IV: You do not have the right to free food and housing. Americans are the most charitable people to be found, and will gladly help anyone in need, but we are quickly growing weary of subsidizing generation after generation of professional couch potatoes who achieve nothing more than the creation of another generation of professional couch potatoes.

ARTICLE V: You do not have the right to free health care. That would be nice, but from the looks of public housing, we're just not interested in public health care.

ARTICLE VI: You do not have the right to physically harm other people. If you kidnap, rape, intentionally maim, or kill someone, don't be surprised if the rest of us want to see you fry in the electric chair.

ARTICLE VII: You do not have the right to the possessions of others. If you rob, cheat or coerce away the goods or services of other citizens, don't be surprised if the rest of us get together and lock you away in a place where you still won't have the right to a big screen color TV or a life of leisure.

ARTICLE VIII: You don't have the right to demand that our children risk their lives in foreign wars to soothe your aching conscience. We hate oppressive governments and won't lift a finger to stop you from going to fight if you'd like. However, we do not enjoy parenting the entire world and do not want to spend so much of our time battling each and every little tyrant with a military uniform and a funny hat.

ARTICLE IX: You don't have the right to a job. All of us sure want all of you to have one, and will gladly help you along in hard times, but we expect you to take advantage of the opportunities of education and vocational training laid before you to make yourself useful.

ARTICLE X: You do not have the right to happiness. Being an American means that you have the right to pursue happiness - which by the way, is a lot easier if you are unencumbered by an overabundance of idiotic laws created by those of you who were confused by the Bill of Rights.

If you agree, we strongly urge you to forward this to as many people as you can. No, you don't have to, and nothing tragic will befall you should you not forward it. We just think it is about time common sense is allowed to flourish - call it the age of reason revisited.

THE ANT AND THE GRASSHOPPER - ORIGINAL VERSION

The ant works hard in the withering heat all summer long, building his House and laying up supplies for the winter. The grasshopper thinks she's a fool and laughs and dances and plays the summer away. Come winter, the ant is warm and well fed. The grasshopper has no food or shelter so he dies out in the cold.

MODERN AMERICAN VERSION - AKA Politically Correct Version

Come winter, the shivering grasshopper calls a press conference and demands to know why the ant should be allowed to be warm and well fed while others are cold and starving. CBS, NBC and ABC show up to provide pictures of the shivering grasshopper next to video of the ant in his comfortable home with a table filled with food. America is stunned by the sharp contrast. How can it be that, in a country of such wealth, this poor grasshopper is allowed to suffer so? Then a representative of the NAGB (The national association of green bugs) shows up on Nightline and charges the ant with green bias, and makes the case that the grasshopper is the victim of 30 million years of greenism.

Kermit the Frog appears on Oprah with the grasshopper, and everybody cries when he sings "It's not easy being green." Bill and Hillary Clinton make a special guest appearance on the CBS Evening News to tell a concerned Dan Rather that they will do everything they can for the grasshopper who has been denied the prosperity he deserves by those who benefited unfairly during the Reagan summers, or as Bill refers to it, the "Temperatures of the 80's." Richard Gephardt exclaims in an interview with Peter Jennings that the ant has gotten rich off the back of the grasshopper and calls for an immediate tax hike on the ant to make him pay his "fair share." Finally, the EC drafts the "Economic Equity and Anti-Greenism Act," retroactive to the beginning of the summer.

The ant is fined for failing to hire a proportionate number of green bugs and, having nothing left to pay his retroactive taxes, his home is confiscated by the government. Hillary gets her old law firm to represent the grasshopper in a defamation suit against the ant, and the case is tried before a panel of federal judges that Bill appointed from a list of single-parent welfare moms who can only hear cases on Thursday's between 1:30 and 3 PM when there are no talk shows scheduled. The ant loses the case.

The story ends as we see the grasshopper finishing up the last bits of the ant's food while the government house he's in, which just happens to be the ant's old house, crumbles around him since he doesn't know how to maintain it. The ant has disappeared in the snow. And on the TV, which the grasshopper bought by selling most of the ant's food, they are showing Bill Clinton standing before a wildly applauding group of Democrats announcing that a new era of "fairness" has dawned in America.

The President of the United States is getting off his helicopter on the lawn of the White House. He has a baby pig under each arm. The Marine Guard snaps to attention and says, "Nice pigs, Sir." The President replies, "These are not pigs, these are authentic Arkansas Razorback Hogs. I got one for Hillary and I got one for Chelsea." The Marine again snaps to attention and replies, "Nice trade, Sir."

The Supreme Court has ruled that there cannot be a nativity scene in Washington, D.C. this Christmas. This isn't for any religious reason. They simply have not been able to find three wise men and a virgin in the Nation's capital. There was no problem however, finding enough asses to fill the stable.

The Office of Personnel Management for the Federal government today announced the 2000 holiday schedule for Federal employees. There will be 2 less holidays in D.C. next year:

Halloween and Thanksgiving

Both will be canceled! The witch is moving to New York and she's taking the turkey with her.

Bill and Hillary were sitting in the bleachers waiting for a baseball game to start. A row of secret service agents sat behind them. One of them leaned forward and whispered something into Bill's ear. Bill turned around, shrugged at the agent, then lifted Hillary by the scruff of the neck and the seat of the pants and tossed her out onto the field. The agent just shook his head and said, "NO, NO, Mr. President," I said, "Throw out the first PITCH."

This is from a contest on Long Island. The requirements were to use the two words, Lewinsky and Kaczynski (the Unabomber), in a limerick. Here are the three winners:

Thirdplace:
There once was a gal named Lewinsky
Who played on a flute like Stravinsky
'Twas "Hail to the Chief"
On this flute made of beef
That stole the front page from Kaczynski.

Secondplace:
Said Clinton to young Ms. Lewinsky
We don't want to leave clues like Kaczynski,
Since you made such a mess,
Use the hem of your dress
And wipe that stuff off your chinsky.
And the winning entry:
Lewinsky and Clinton have shown
What Kaczynski must surely have known:
That an intern is better
Than a bomb in a letter
When deciding how best to be blown.

George W. Bush, in an airport lobby, noticed a man in a long flowing white robe with a long flowing white beard and flowing white hair. The man had a staff in one hand and some stone tablets under the other arm. George W. approached the man and inquired, "Aren't you Moses." The man ignored George W. and stared at the ceiling. George W. positioned himself more directly in the man's view and asked again, "Aren't you Moses". The man continued to peruse the ceiling.

George W. tugged at the man's sleeve and asked once again, "Aren't you Moses". The man finally responded in an irritated voice, "Yes I am".

George W. asked him why he was so uppity and the man replied, "The last time I spoke to a Bush I had to spend forty years in the desert".

Lord,
Grant me the serenity
to
Accept the things
I cannot change,
the Courage to
Change the things I can
and the wisdom
to hide the bodies of
those people I had to
kill because they
flat pissed
me off!

Dear Lord,

So far today, God, I've done all right. I haven't gossiped, haven't lost my temper, haven't been greedy, grumpy, nasty, selfish, or over-indulgent. I'm really glad about that. But . . .

In a few minutes, God, I'm going to get out of bed, and from then on I'm probably going to need a lot more help.

Thank you. Amen

A LETTER TO GOD

A little boy who wanted $100 very badly prayed and prayed for two weeks but nothing happened. Then he decided to write God a letter requesting the $100.

When the US Postal Service authorities received the letter to "GOD, USA," they decided to send it to the president. The president was so impressed, touched, and amused, that he instructed his secretary to send the little boy a $5 bill. The president thought that this would appear to be a lot of money to a little boy.

The little boy was so delighted with the $5 that he immediately sat down to write a thank-you note to God which read:

"Dear God: Thank you very much for sending me the money. However, I noticed that for some reason you had to send it through Washington DC and, as usual, those bastards kept 95%."

The Rescue Mission

Rev. Duane A Martin
123 Temperance Avenue
Mars, Pennsylvania 16046

Dear Sir,

Perhaps you have heard of my Nationwide Campaign in the cause of temperance. Each year for the past fourteen years, I have made a tour of Indiana, Texas, Virginia, Wyoming, California, Colorado and Tennessee, and have delivered a series of lectures on the "Evils of Drinking." On this tour I have been accompanied by a young man, a personal friend of mine, who has assisted me in my many lectures. His name is Clyde Lindstrome. Clyde, a young man of good family and excellent background, is a pathetic example of life ruined by excessive indulgence in whiskey and women.

Clyde would appear with me at the lectures and sit on the platform, wheezing and staring at the audience through bleary, blood-shot eyes, sweating profusely, picking his nose, passing gas, and making obscene gestures, while I would point him out as an example of what over-indulgence can do to a person.

I deeply regret that Clyde past away last fall. A mutual friend has given me your name and I wonder if you would be available to take Clyde's place on my next Winter and Spring Tour?

I will be looking forward to your reply.

Yours in Faith,

Reverend Duane A Martin

The Rescue Mission

THE PRIEST

The young Priest, at his first Mass, was so afraid he could hardly speak. So, before his second week in the pulpit, he asked the Monsignor how he could relax. The Monsignor (a veteran at his work) said, "My Son, this Sunday it might help if you put a martini in the water pitcher instead of water. After a few sips, everything should go smoothly."

So Sunday came and the young Priest did as the Monsignor had suggested and he could really talk up a storm. After the sermon, the young Priest asked the Monsignor how he had done. The Monsignor replied, "Just fine, except you should remember the following before addressing the congregation again":

1. Next time, sip the martini rather than gulp it by the glassful.

2. There are 10 commandments, not 12.

3. There are 12 disciples, not 10.

4. David slew Goliath, he didn't kick the crap out of him.

5. The recommended grace before a meal is not 'Rub-A-Dub-Dub, thanks for the grub.'

6. Do not refer to our Savior Jesus Christ and his Disciples as "J.C. and the boys."

7. We don't refer to the Cross as the "Big T."

8. We don't refer to the Father, Son and Holy Ghost as "Big Daddy, Junior and the Spook."

9. Next Sunday, there is a taffy pulling contest at St. Peter's, not a peter pulling contest at St. Taffy's.

10. Last, but not least, we say "The Virgin Mary", not "Mary with the cherry!"

ATTENTION

The Occupational Safety & Health Administration (OSHA) has determined that the maximum safe load capacity on my butt is 2 persons at a time-- unless I install handrails or safety straps.

As you have arrived 8th in line to ride my ass, please take a number and wait your turn.

TO: ALL EMPLOYEES
FROM: MANAGEMENT
Re: REVISED RETIREMENT PLAN

As a result of the reduction of money budgeted for departmental areas, we are forced to cut down on our number of personnel.

Under this revised plan, older employees will be asked to go on early retirement, thus permitting the retention of the younger people who represent our future.

Therefore, a program to phase out personnel by the end of the current fiscal year, via retirement, will be placed into effect immediately. This program will be known as Retire Aged Personnel Early (RAPE).

Employees who are RAPED will be given the opportunity to look for other jobs outside the company. Provided that they are RAPED, they can request a review of their employment records before actual retirement takes place. This phase of operation is called Survey of Capabilities of Retired Early Workers (SCREW).

All employees who have been RAPED or SCREWED may file an appeal with upper management. This phase is called Study by Higher Authority Following Termination (SHAFT). Under the terms of the new policy, an employee may be RAPED once, SCREWED twice, but may be SHAFTED as many times as the company deems appropriate.

If an employee follows the above procedures, he/she will be entitled to Half Earnings for Retired Personnel Early Severance (HERPES) or Combined Lump-sum Assistance Payment (CLAP), unless he/she already has Additional Income from Dependent or Spouse (AIDS). As HERPES and CLAP are considered benefit plans, any employee who has received HERPES or CLAP will no longer be RAPED or SCREWED by the company.

Management wishes to assure the younger employees who remain on board that the company will continue its policy to ensure that employees are well trained through our Special High Intensity Training (SHIT). The company takes pride in the amount of SHIT our employees receive. We have given our employees more SHIT than any other company in this area. If any employee feels he/she does not receive enough SHIT on the job, see your immediate supervisor. Your supervisor is especially trained to make sure that you receive ALL the SHIT you can stand.

MEMO TO: All Employees
Subject: Employee Development

The Specialized High Intensity Training (SHIT) Program has been canceled due to lack of interest.

Below is a partial list of substitute classes being offered to all employees beginning in the Fall. Please indicate your 1st, 2nd and 3rd choice and return to the Employee Training Support Division no later than Friday of this week. A summary of your selections will be prepared to determine the overall interest for the class justification and training requirements.

SELF IMPROVEMENT:

101-A Creative Suffering
101-B Overcoming Peace of Mind
102-A Guilt without Sex
102-B Ego Gratification Through Violence
103-A A New Drug to Enhance Your Social life
103-B The Art of Indecision
104-A Creative Depression
104-B Whine Your Way to Alienation
105-A How to Overcome Self Doubt Through Pretense and Ostentation

BUSINESS AND CAREER

106-A Money Can Make You Rich
106-B How I Made $100 in Real Estate
107-A Career Opportunities in El Salvador
107-B How to Profit From Your Own Body

108-A The Underachiever's Guide to Very Small Business Opportunities
108-B Looter's Guide to America's Cities
109-A Growing Grass for Fun and Profit
109-B How to maximize your losses

HOME ECONOMICS:

201-A How You Can Convert Your Family
       Room into a Garage
202-A What to do with Your Conversation Pit
202-B 1001 Other Uses for Your Vacuum Cleaner
203-A Burglarproof Your Home with concrete
203-B The Repair and Maintenance of your Virginity
204-A How to Convert a Wheelchair into a Dune Buggy
204-B Christianity and the Art of RV Vehicle Maintenance

HEALTH AND FITNESS

205-A Creative Tooth Decay
205-B Exorcism and Acne
206-A The Joys of Hypochondria
206-B High Fiber Sex
207-A Biofeedback and How to Stop it
207-B Skate Yourself to Regularity
208-A Understanding Nudity
208-B Tap Dance Your Way to Social Ridicule
209-A Optimum Body Functions

CRAFTS

209-B Self-Actualization Through Macramé
301-A How to Draw Genitalia
301-B Needlecraft for Junkies
302-A How to Bonsai your Pet
302-B Gifts for the Senile
303-A How to Wok your dog

NewWorkPolicies
From: Management
Effective: Immediately (or Sooner)

SICK DAYS:
We will no longer accept a doctor statement as proof of sickness. If you are able to go to the doctor, you are able to come to work.

SURGERY:
Operations are now banned. As long as you are an employee here, you need all your organs. You should not consider removing anything. We hired you intact. To have something removed constitutes a breach of employment.

PERSONAL DAYS:
Each employee will receive 104 personal days a year. They are called Saturday & Sunday.

VACATION DAYS:
All employees will take their vacation at the same time every year. The vacation days are as follows: Jan. 1, July 4 & Dec. 25

BEREAVEMENT LEAVE:
This is no excuse for missing work. There is nothing you can do for dead friends, relatives or coworkers. Every effort should be made to have non-employees attend to the arrangements. In rare cases where employee involvement is necessary, the funeral should be scheduled in the late afternoon. We will be glad to allow you to work through your lunch hour and subsequently leave one hour early, provided your share of the work is done.

OUT FOR YOUR OWN DEATH:
This will be accepted as an excuse. However, we require at least two-weeks-notice as it is your duty to train your own replacement.

LUNCH BREAK:
Skinny people get an hour for lunch as they need to eat more so that they can look healthy; normal sized people get 30 minutes for lunch to get a balanced meal to maintain the average figure; fat people get 5 minutes for lunch because that's all the time needed to drink a Slim Fast & take a diet pill.

DRESS CODE:
It is advised that you come to work dressed according to your salary. If we see you wearing $350 Prada sneakers & carrying a $600 Gucci bag, we assume you are doing well financially and therefore you do not need a raise.

Thank you for your loyalty to our company. We are here to provide a positive employment experience. Therefore, all questions, comments, concerns, complaints, frustrations, irritations, aggravations, insinuations, allegations, accusations, contemplations, consternations or input, should be directed elsewhere. Have a nice week.

Retirement

My nookie days are over,

My pilot light is out.

What used to be my sex appeal

Is now my water spout.

Time was when of its own accord,

From my trousers it would spring.

But now I have a full time job

Just to find the blasted thing.

It used to be embarrassing,

The way it would behave.

For every single morning,

It would stand and watch me shave.

As old age approaches,

It sure gives me the blues

To see it hang its withered head

And watch me tie my shoes.

My Forgetter's Getting Better: Author Unkown

My forgetter's getting better
But my rememberer is broke
To you that may seem funny
But, to me, it is no joke.

For when I'm "here" I'm wondering
If I really should be "there"
And, when I try to think it through,
I haven't got a prayer!

Oft times I walk into a room,
and Say "what am I in here for?"
I wrack my brain, but all in vain
A zero, is my score.

At times I put something away
Where it is safe, but, gee!
The person it is safest from
Is, generally, me!

When shopping I may see someone,
Say "Hi" and have a chat,
Then, when the person walks away
I ask myself, "who's that?"

Yes, my forgetter's getting better
While my rememberer is broke,
And it's driving me plumb crazy
And that isn't any joke.

HOW TO SING THE BLUES – Received off of email, no authorship given:

1. Most Blues begin, "Woke up this morning."

2. "I got a good woman" is a bad way to begin the Blues, 'less you stick something nasty in the next line, like " I got a good woman, with the meanest face in town."

3. The Blues is simple. After you get the first line right, repeat it. Then find something that rhymes? sort of: "Got a good woman - with the meanest face in town. Got teeth like Margaret Thatcher - and she weigh 500 pound."

4. The Blues are not about choice. You stuck in a ditch, you stuck in a ditch; ain't no way out.

5. Blues cars: Chevys and Cadillacs and broken-down trucks. Blues don't travel in Volvos, BMWs, or Sport Utility Vehicles. Most Blues transportation is a Greyhound bus or a southbound train. Jet aircraft an' state-sponsored motor pools ain't even in the running. Walkin' plays a major part in the blues lifestyle. So does fixin' to die.

6. Teenagers can't sing the Blues. They ain't fixin' to die yet. Adults sing the Blues. In Blues, "adulthood" means being old enough to get the electric chair if you shoot a man in Memphis.

7. Blues can take place in New York City but not in Hawaii or any place in Canada. Hard times in St. Paul or Tucson is just depression. Chicago, St. Louis, and Kansas City still the best places to have the Blues. You cannot have the blues in any place that don't get rain.

8. A man with male pattern baldness ain't the blues. A woman with male pattern baldness is. Breaking your leg cuz you skiing is not the blues. Breaking your leg cuz an alligator be chomping on it is.

9. You can't have no Blues in an office or a shopping mall. The lighting is wrong. Go outside to the parking lot or sit by the dumpster.

10. Good places for the Blues:
a. highway
b. jailhouse
c. empty bed
d. bottom of a whiskey glass

Bad places:
a. Ashrams
b. gallery openings
c. Ivy League institutions
d. golf courses

11. No one will believe it's the Blues if you wear a suit, 'less you happen to be an old ethnic person, and you slept in it.

12. Do you have the right to sing the Blues?

Yes, if:
a. you're older than dirt
b. you're blind
c. you shot a man in Memphis
d. you can't be satisfied

No, if:
a. you have all your teeth
b. you were once blind but now can see
c. the man in Memphis lived.
d. you have a retirement plan or trust fund.

13. Blues is not a matter of color. It's a matter of bad luck. Tiger Woods cannot sing the blues. Gary Coleman could. Ugly white people also got a leg up on the blues.

14. If you ask for water and Baby give you gasoline, it's the Blues. Other acceptable Blues beverages are:
a. wine
b. whiskey or bourbon
c. muddy water
d. black coffee

The following are NOT Blues beverages:
a. mixed drinks
b. kosher wine
c. Snapple
d. sparkling water

15. If it occurs in a cheap motel or a shotgun shack, it's a Blues death. Stabbed in the back by a jealous lover is another Blues way to die. So is the electric chair, substance abuse, and dying lonely on a broken -own cot.
You can't have a Blues death if you die during a tennis match or getting liposuction.

16. Some Blues names for women:
a. Sadie
b. Big Mama
c. Bessie
d. Fat River Dumpling

17. Some Blues names for men:
a. Joe
b. Willie
c. Little Willie
d. Big Willie

18. Persons with names like Sierra, Sequoia, Auburn, and Rainbow can't sing the Blues no matter how many men they shoot in Memphis.

19. Make your own Blues name (starter kit):
a. name of physical infirmity (Blind, Cripple, Lame, etc.)
b. first name (see above) plus name of fruit (Lemon, Lime, Kiwi, etc.)
c. Last name of President (Jefferson, Johnson, Fillmore, etc.)

For example, Blind Lime Jefferson, or Cripple Kiwi Fillmore, etc. (Well, maybe not "Kiwi.")

20. I don't care how tragic your life; you own a computer. You cannot sing the blues. You best destroy it. Fire, a spilled bottle of Mad Dog, or get out a shotgun. Maybe your big woman just done sat on it. I don't care.

SIGNS THAT YOU ARE NO LONGER A KID

You're asleep, but others worry that you're dead.
Your back goes out more than you do.
You quit trying to hold your stomach in, no matter who walks into the room.
You buy a compass for the dash of your car.
You are proud of your lawn mower.
Your best friend is dating someone half their age, and isn't breaking any laws.
Your arms are almost too short to read the newspaper.
You sing along with the elevator music.
You would rather go to work than stay home sick.
You constantly talk about the price of gasoline.
You enjoy hearing about other people's operations.
You consider coffee one of the most important things in life.
You no longer think of speed limits as a challenge.
Neighbors borrow *your* tools.
People call at 9 p.m. and ask, "Did I wake you?"
You have a dream about prunes.
You answer a question with, "because I said so!"
You send money to PBS.
The end of your tie doesn't come anywhere near the top of your pants.
You take a metal detector to the beach.

You wear black socks with sandals.

You know what the word "equity" means.

You can't remember the last time you laid on the floor to watch television.

Your ears are hairier than your head.

You get into a heated argument about pension plans.

You got cable for the weather channel.

(the Weather Channel also known as "Old Folks MTV.")

You can go bowling without drinking.

You have a party and the neighbors & don't even realize it.

ANNOUNCING:
SEMINARS FOR MEN

COURSE 001:Combating Stupidity

COURSE 002:You Too Can Do Housework

COURSE 003:PMS -- Learn When to Keep Your Mouth Shut

COURSE 004:How to Fill an Ice Tray

COURSE 005:We Do Not Want Sleazy Under things for Christmas

COURSE 006:Wonderful Laundry Techniques (formerly: Don't Wash My Silks)

COURSE 007:Understanding the Female Response to Coming Home at 4:00 AM

COURSE 008:Parenting: It Doesn't End with Conception

COURSE 009:Get a Life: Learn to Cook

COURSE 010:How Not to Look Like an Asshole When You are Obviously Wrong

COURSE 011:Understanding Your Incompetence

COURSE 012:YOU: The Weaker Sex

COURSE 013:Reasons to Give Flowers

COURSE 014:How to Stay Awake After Sex

COURSE 015:SEX 101: You Can Fall Asleep Without it if You Really Try

COURSE 016:SEX 102: Morning Dilemma - If IT'S Awake, Take a Shower

COURSE 017:How to Put Down the Toilet Seat

COURSE 018:Remote Control: Overcoming Your Dependency

COURSE 019: How NOT to Act Younger than Your Children
COURSE 020: You Too Can be a Designated Driver
COURSE 021: Honest - You Don't Look Like Mel Gibson - Especially Naked
COURSE 022: The Obtainable Goal: Omitting *$&#%%# From Your Vocabulary
COURSE 023: Fluffing the Blanket After Farting is Not Necessary
COURSE 024: Real Men Ask for Directions
COURSE 025: How NOT to Forget Birthdays, Anniversaries, Valentines Day, etc.

Please register immediately as courses are in great demand. Class size will be limited to 10 as course material may prove difficult.

Additional Training Courses Available for Men:

1. Introduction to Common Household Objects I: The Mop
2. Introduction to Common Household Objects II: The Sponge
3. Dressing Up: Beyond the Funeral and the Wedding
4. Refrigerator Forensics: Identifying and Removing the Dead (Lori)
5. Design Pattern or Splatter Stain on the Linoleum? You CAN Tell the Difference!
6. If It's Empty, You Can Throw It Away: Accepting Loss I
7. If the Milk Expired Three Weeks Ago, Keeping It In the Refrigerator Won't Bring It Back: Accepting Loss II
8. Going to the Supermarket: It's Not Just for Women Anymore!
9. Recycling Skills I: Boxes that the Electronics Came In
10. Recycling Skills II: Styrofoam that Came in the Boxes that the Electronics Came in
11. Bathroom Etiquette I: How to Remove Beard Clippings from the Sink
12. Bathroom Etiquette II: Let's Wash Those Towels!
13. Bathroom Etiquette III: Five Easy Ways to Tell When You're About to Run Out of Toilet Paper!
14. Giving Back to the Community: How to Donate 15-Year-Old Levis to the Goodwill (Lori)

15. Retro? Or Just Hideous? Re-examining Your 1970s Polyester Shirts

16. No, The Dishes Won't Wash Themselves: Knowing the Limitations of Your Kitchenware

17. Romance: More Than a Cable Channel!

18. Strange But True! She Really May NOT Care What "Fourth Down and Ten" Means (Ha, I DO know!)

19. Going Out to Dinner: Beyond the Pizza Hut

20. Expand Your Entertainment Options: Renting Movies That Don't Fall Under the "Action/ Adventure" Category

21. Yours, Mine, and Ours: Sharing the Remote

22. "I Could Have Played a Better Game Than That!": Why Women Laugh

23. Adventures in Housekeeping I: Let's Clean the Closet (Lori)

24. Adventures in Housekeeping II: Let's Clean Under the Bed (Lori)

25. "I Don't Know": Be the First Man to Say It!

26. The Gas Gauge in Your Car: Sometimes Empty MEANS Empty (Lori)

27. Directions: It's Okay to Ask for Them

28. Listening: It's Not Just Something You Do During Half-time

29. Accepting Your Limitations: Just Because You Have Power Tools Doesn't Mean You Can Fix It

ANNOUNCING:
SEMINARS FOR WOMEN

COURSE 001: Silence, The Final Frontier: Where no woman has gone.
COURSE 002: The Undiscovered Side Of Banking: Making deposits.
COURSE 003: Parties: Going without new outfits.
COURSE 004: Man Management: Discover how minor household chores can wait until after the game.
COURSE 005: Learning To Go In Public Rest rooms.

COURSE 006: PMS: Your problem ... not his.
COURSE 007: Communication Skills I: Tears - the last resort, not the first.
COURSE 008: Communication Skills II: Thinking before speaking.
COURSE 009: Communication Skills III: Getting what you want without nagging.
COURSE 010: Driving A Car Safely: A skill you CAN acquire.

COURSE 011: Telephone Skills: How to hang up.
COURSE 012: Introduction to Parking.
COURSE 013: Advanced Parking: Reversing into a space.
COURSE 014: Water Retention: Fact or fat.
COURSE 015: Integrating Your Laundry: Washing it all together.

COURSE 016: Cooking I: Bringing back bacon, eggs and butter.
COURSE 017: Cooking II: Bran and tofu are not for human consumption.
COURSE 018: Cooking III: How not to inflict your diets on other people.
COURSE 019: "Do these jeans make my butt look big?" - Why men lie.
COURSE 020: Compliments: Accepting them gracefully.

COURSE 021: Honest - You Don't Look Like Vanna White - Especially Naked

COURSE 022: Bathroom Etiquette I: Men need space in the bathroom cabinet too.

COURSE 023: Bathroom Etiquette II: His razor is HIS.

COURSE 024: Oil & Petrol: Your car needs both.

COURSE 025: Oil & Petrol: Your car needs both. (in case it was missed the first time).

Please register immediately as courses are in great demand. Class size will be limited to 10 as course material may prove difficult.

Things only Women Understand:

PREGNANCY Q & A

Q: Should I have a baby after 35?
A: No, 35 children is enough.

Q: I'm two months pregnant now. When will my baby move?
A: With any luck, right after he finishes college.

Q: What is the most reliable method to determine a baby's sex?
A: Childbirth.

Q: My wife is five months pregnant and so moody that sometimes she's borderline irrational.
A: So what's your question?

Q: My childbirth instructor says it's not pain I'll feel during labor, but pressure. Is she right?
A: Yes, in the same way that a tornado might be called an air current.

Q: When is the best time to get an epidural?
A: Right after you find out you're pregnant.

Q: Is there any reason I have to be in the delivery room while my wife is in labor?
A: Not unless the word "alimony" means anything to you.

Q: Is there anything I should avoid while recovering from childbirth?
A: Yes, pregnancy.

Q: Do I have to have a baby shower?
A: Not if you change the baby's diaper very quickly.

Q: Our baby was born last week. When will my wife begin to feel and act normal again?
A: When the kids are in college.

The Top Ten Lists:

10 WAYS TO KNOW IF YOU HAVE "ESTROGEN ISSUES"
1. Everyone around you has an attitude problem.
2. You're adding chocolate chips to your cheese omelet.
3. The dryer has shrunk every last pair of your jeans.
4. Your husband is suddenly agreeing to everything you say.
5. You're using your cellular phone to dial up every bumper sticker that says: "How's my driving-call 1-800-***-."
6. Everyone's head looks like an invitation to batting-practice.
7. You're convinced there's a God and he's male.
8. You can't believe they don't make a tampon bigger than Super Plus.
9. You're sure that everyone is scheming to drive you crazy.
10. The ibuprofen bottle is empty and you bought it yesterday.

TOP TEN THINGS ONLY WOMEN UNDERSTAND
10. Cats' facial expressions.
9. The need for the same style of shoes in different colors.
8. Why bean sprouts aren't just weeds.
7. Fat clothes.
6. Taking a car trip without trying to beat your best time.

5. The difference between beige, ecru, cream, off-white, and eggshell.

4. Cutting your fringe to make it grow.

3. Eyelash curlers.

2. The inaccuracy of every bathroom scale ever made.

AND, the Number One thing only women understand:

1. OTHER WOMEN

Top Ten Things NEVER to Say To A Woman During An Argument:

10. "Don't you have some laundry to do or something?"

9. "Oh, you are so cute when you get all pissed off."

8. "You're just upset because your ass is beginning to spread."

7. "Wait a minute...I get it -- what time of the month is it?"

6. "You sure you don't want to consult the Great Oprah on this one?"

5. "Sorry. I was just picturing you naked."

4. "Whoa, time out, honey. Football is on."

3. "Looks like someone had an extra bowl of Bitch Flakes this morning."

2. "Is there any way we can do this via e-mail?"

THE #1 THING YOU SHOULD NEVER SAY TO A WOMAN DURING AN ARGUMENT...

"Who are you kidding? We both know that thing ain't loaded."

Top 20 things NOT to Say During Sex!

20. "But everybody looks funny naked!"
19. "Biege, I think I'll change the ceiling color to beige."
18. "Oh, did you make a deposit at the bank today?"
17. "Did I mention the video camera?"
16. "Do you smell something burning?"
15. "You woke me up for that?"
14. "And to think, I was really trying to pick up your friend!"
13. "Hope you're as good looking when I'm sober."
12. "Maybe we should call Dr. Ruth."
11. "Sweetheart, did you lock the back door?"
10. "Smile, you're on Candid Camera!"
9. "Have you seen "Fatal Attraction"?"
8. "Maybe you're just out of practice."
7. "On second thought, let's turn off the lights."
6. "It's nice being in bed with a woman I don't have to inflate!"
5. "You're almost as good as my ex!"
4. "And to think, I didn't even have to buy you dinner!"
3. "Did I tell you my Aunt Martha died in this bed?"
2. "Does this count as a date?"
1. "I really hate women who actually think sex means something!"

NOTICE
TO ALL EMPLOYEES

It has been brought to management's attention that some individuals have been using foul language in the course of normal conversation among employees. Due to complaints from some of the more easily offended workers, this conduct will no longer be tolerated.

The management realizes, however, the importance of each person being able to properly express their feelings when communicating with their fellow employees. Therefore, the management has compiled the following code phrases, so that the proper exchange of ideas and information may continue.

OLD PHRASE	NEW PHRASE
1. No Fucking way.	1. I'm not certain that's feasible.
2. You've got to be shitting me.	2. Really.
3. Tell someone who gives a shit.	3. Perhaps you should check with...
4. Ask me if I give a shit.	4. Of course I'm concerned.
5. It's not my fucking problem.	5. I wasn't involved with that project.
6. What the hell???	6. Interesting behavior
7. Screw it. It won't work.	7. I'm not sure I can implement this.
8. Why the hell didn't you tell me sooner?	8. I'll try to schedule that.
9. When the hell do you expect me to do it?	9. Perhaps I can work late.
10. Who the hell cares?	10. Are you sure it's a problem?
11. He's got his head up his ass.	11. He's not familiar with the problem
12. Eat shit.	12. You don't say.
13. Eat shit and die.	13. Excuse me?
14. Eat shit and die ass hole.	4. Excuse me, sir?
15. What the hell do they want from me?	15. They weren't happy with it?
16. Kiss my ass.	16. So you'd like my help with it?
17. Screw it. I'm on salary.	17. I'm a bit overloaded at the moment.
18. Shove it up your ass.	18. I don't think you understand.
19. This fucking job sucks.	19. I love a challenge.
20. Who the hell died and left you boss ?	20. Do you want me to take care of this?
21. Blow me.	21. I see.
22. Blow yourself.	22. Do you see?
23. Another fucking meeting.	23. Yes, we should discuss this.
24. I really don't give a shit.	24. I don't think it will be a problem.
25. Hey shit for brains!	25. Let's think this through.

At work, don't you wish you could say.......

Do I look like a people person?
What am I? Flypaper for freaks!?
If I throw a stick, will you leave?
I don't work here. I'm a consultant.
How do I set a laser printer to stun?
How about never? Is never good for you?
I thought I was wrong but I was mistaken.
Sarcasm is just one more service we offer.
Does your train of thought have a caboose?
I pretend to work. They pretend to pay me.
Well, this day was a total waste of makeup.
Errors have been made. Others will be blamed.
I'm trying to imagine you with a personality.
I'm not being rude. You're just insignificant.
Chaos, panic & disorder - my work here is done.
Can I trade this job for what's behind door #1?
A cubicle is just a padded cell without a door.
And your crybaby whiny-butt opinion would be...?
I'll try being nicer if you'll try being smarter.
I'm out of my mind, but feel free to leave a message.
You are validating my inherent mistrust of strangers.
Whatever kind of look you were going for, you missed.
I'm already visualizing the duct tape over your mouth.
Ahhh...I see the screw-up fairy has visited us again...
I started out with nothing & still have most of it left.
According to my calculations, the problem doesn't exist.
I Refuse To Have A Battle Of Wits With An Unarmed Person.
I like you. You remind me of when I was young and stupid.
This isn't an office. It's Hell with fluorescent lighting.
I have plenty of talent and vision. I just don't give a damn.
I can see your point, but I still think you are full of shit.
It's a thankless job, but I've got a lot of Karma to burn off.
I thought I wanted a career, turns out I just wanted paychecks.
I will always cherish the initial misconceptions I had about you.

Yes, I am an agent of Satan, but my duties are largely ceremonial.

The fact that no one understands you doesn't mean you're an artist.

Any connection between your reality and mine is purely coincidental.

I don't know what your problem is, but I'll bet it's hard to pronounce..

I see you've set aside this special time to humiliate yourself in public.

I'm really easy to get along with once you people learn to see it my way.

Thank you. We're all refreshed and challenged by your unique point of view.

Fifteen Words that don't, but should exist:

1. Arachnoleptic fit (n.) The frantic dance performed when a spider drops onto your lap.
2. Beelzebug (n.) Satan in the form of a mosquito that gets into your bedroom at 3 in the morning and cannot be cast out.
3. Bozone (n.) The substance surrounding stupid people that stops bright ideas from penetrating. The bozone layer, unfortunately, shows little sign of breaking down in the near future. ...does this remind anyone of one of the rooms in L-10? The one which appears to have a high Bozone reading?
4. Cashtration (n.) The act of buying a house, which renders the subject financially impotent for an indefinite period.
5. Caterpallor (n.) The color you turn after finding half a grub in the fruit you're eating.
6. Decaflon (n.) The grueling event of getting through the day consuming only things that are good for you.
7. Dopelar effect (n.) The tendency of stupid ideas to seem smarter when you come at them rapidly.
8. Extraterrestaurant (n.) An eating place where you feel you've been abducted and experimented upon. La Belvedere, for example.
9. Faunacated (adj.) How wildlife ends up when its environment is destroyed. Hence faunacatering (n.), which has made a meal of many species.
10. Foreploy (n.) Any misrepresentation or outright lie about yourself that leads to sex.
11. Grantartica (n.) The cold, isolated place where arts companies without funding dwell.
12. Hemaglobe (n.) The bloody state of the world.
13. Intaxication (n.) Euphoria at getting a tax refund, which lasts until you realize it was your money to start with.
14. Kinstirpation (n.) A painful inability to move relatives who come to visit.
15. Lullabuoy (n.) An idea that keeps floating into your head and prevents you from drifting off to sleep.

An organization is like a tree full of monkeys,... all on different limbs,... at different levels,...some climbing up. The monkeys on the top look down and see a tree full of smiling faces. The monkeys on the bottom look up and see nothing but assholes.

YOU KNOW YOU'RE TOO STRESSED IF...

Relatives that have been dead for years come visit you and suggest that you should get some rest.
You can achieve a "Runners High" by sitting up.
You say the same sentence over and over again, not realizing that you have said it before.
The Sun is too loud.
Trees begin chasing you.
You can see individual air molecules vibrating.
You begin to explore the possibility of setting up an I. V. drip solution of espresso.
You wonder if brewing is really a necessary step for the consumption of coffee.
You can hear mimes.
You believe that if you think hard enough, you can fly.
Things becomes "Very Clear".
You ask the drive-thru attendant if you can get your order to go.
You say the same sentence over and over again, not realizing that you have said it before...
You begin speaking in a language that only you and those who channel can understand.
The less sense matter and matter is more than sense.
You keep yelling "STOP TOUCHING ME!!!" even If you are the only one in the room.
Your heart beats in 7/8 time.
You and Reality file for divorce.
You can skip without a rope.
It appears that people are speaking to you in binary code.
You have great revelations concerning: Life, the Universe, and Everything else, but can't quite find the words for them before the white glow disappear, leaving you more confused than before.

You can travel without moving.

Antacid tablets become your sole source of nutrition.

You discover the aesthetic beauty of office supplies.

You have an irresistible urge to bite the noses of the people you are talking to.

You say the same sentence over and over again, not realizing that you have said it before...

Losing your mind was okay, but when the voices in your head quieted, it was like losing your best friend.

Accident, Poor Planning!

A man sent a letter to his insurance company stating that the cause of his accident was poor planning. The insurance company sent him back a letter stating, "Could you please elaborate?" He sent a reply stating, "I hope the following will be sufficient!"

I am a brick layer by trade and on the date of the accident I was working on the top of a six- story building. I had 500 pounds of bricks left over at the end of the day that I had to lower to the ground level. So I used a barrel a rope and a pulley, which fortunately was attached to the side of the building.

I went down to the ground level, tied the rope, went up to the top level and loaded the 500 pounds of bricks into the barrel, swung it out, then went down to the ground level. I untied the rope, securing it tightly to assure a slow descent of the bricks. I refer you to block number 11 of the accident reporting form. I only weigh 125 pounds!

As you can imagine, I began a rather fast ascent up the side of the building. Being jerked off the ground at such a rate of speed, I lost my presence of mind and forgot to let go of the rope. I met the barrel in the vicinity of the third floor, which accounts for my fractured skull and broken collar bone. I didn't stop, however, until I was three knuckles deep into the pulley.

Approximately the same time, the barrel of bricks hit the ground. The bottom fell out of the barrel. Being devoid of the weight of the bricks, the barrel now weighed 50 pounds. I refer you again to block number 11 of the accident reporting form. As you can imagine, I began a rather fast descent down the side of the building. I met the barrel in the vicinity of the third floor, which accounts for the lacerations of my legs and lower body, which slowed my descent so that fortunately, when I fell into the pile of bricks below, only three vertebrae were cracked.

I regret to inform you, however, as I lay there in pain, unable to move, looking at the barrel six stories above me, I again lost my presence of mind and let go of the rope!

No Authorship Given

WARNING - Tazer Guns!

Last weekend I saw something at The Gun Show that sparked my interest. I was looking for a little something different for my wife Dana. What I came across was a 100,000-volt, pocket/purse-sized Tazer.

The effects of the Tazer were supposed to be short lived, with no long term adverse affect on your assailant, allowing her adequate time to retreat to safety...??

WAY TOO COOL! Long story short, I bought the device and brought it home.. I loaded two AAA batteries in the darn thing and pushed the button. Nothing! I was disappointed I learned, however, that if I pushed the button and pressed it against a metal surface at the same time, I'd get the blue arc of electricity darting back and forth between the prongs.

AWESOME!!! Unfortunately, I have yet to explain to Dana what that burn spot is on the face of her microwave.

Okay, so I was home alone with this new toy, thinking to myself that it couldn't be all that bad with only two AAA batteries, right?

There I sat in my recliner, my cat Leo looking on intently (trusting little soul) while I was reading the directions and thinking that I really needed to try this thing out on a flesh & blood moving target.

I must admit I thought about zapping Leo (for a fraction of a second) and then thought better of it. He is such a sweet cat. But, if I was going to give this thing to my wife to protect herself against a mugger, I did want some assurance that it would work as advertised.

Am I wrong?

So, there I sat in a pair of shorts and a singlet with my reading glasses perched delicately on the bridge of my nose, directions in one hand, and Tazer in another.

The directions said that:

A one-second burst would shock and disorient your assailant;

A two-second burst was supposed to cause muscle spasms and a major loss of bodily control; and

A three-second burst would purportedly make your assailant flop on the ground like a fish out of water.

Any burst longer than three seconds would be wasting the batteries.

All the while I'm looking at this little device measuring about 5" long, less than 3/4 inch in circumference (loaded with two itsy, bitsy AAA batteries); pretty cute really, and thinking to myself, 'no possible way!'

What happened next is almost beyond description, but I'll do my best.

I'm sitting there alone, the cat looking on with his head cocked to one side so as to say, 'Don't do it stupid,' reasoning that a one second burst from such a tiny lil ole thing couldn't hurt all that bad.. I decided to give myself a one second burst just for heck of it.

I touched the prongs to my naked thigh, pushed the button, and...

No Authorship Given

HOLY MOTHER OF GOD. WEAPONS OF MASS DESTRUCTION. WHAT THE . . .!!!

I'm pretty sure Hulk Hogan ran in through the side door, picked me up in the recliner, then body slammed us both on the carpet, over and over and over again. I vaguely recall waking up on my side in the fetal position, with tears in my eyes, body soaking wet, both nipples on fire, testicles nowhere to be found, with my left arm tucked under my body in the oddest position, and tingling in my legs! The cat was making meowing sounds I had never heard before, clinging to a picture frame hanging above the fireplace, obviously in an attempt to avoid getting slammed by my body flopping all over the living room.

Note:

If you ever feel compelled to 'mug' yourself with a Tazer,, one note of caution:

There is NO such thing as a one second burst when you zap yourself! You will not let go of that thing until it is dislodged from your hand by a violent thrashing about on the floor! A three second burst would be considered conservative!

A minute or so later (I can't be sure, as time was a relative thing at that point), I collected my wits (what little I had left), sat up and surveyed the landscape.

· My bent reading glasses were on the top of the TV.

· The recliner was upside down and about 8 feet or so from where it originally was.

· My triceps, right thigh and both nipples were still twitching.

· My face felt like it had been shot up with Novocain, and my bottom lip weighed 88 lbs.

· I had no control over the drooling.

· Apparently I had crapped in my shorts, but was too numb to know for sure, and my sense of smell was gone.

· I saw a faint smoke cloud above my head, which I believe came from my hair.

I'm still looking for my testicles and I'm offering a significant reward for their safe return!

PS: My wife can't stop laughing about my experience, loved the gift and now regularly threatens me with it!

ERNIE THE HAMSTER

If you have raised kids (or been one), and gone through the pet syndrome including toilet-flush burials for dead goldfish it's a long story but one that will make you laugh.

Overview: I had to take my son's hamster to the vet. Here's what happened:

Just after dinner one night, my son came up to tell me there was something wrong with one of the two hamsters he holds prisoner in his room. "He's just lying there looking sick," he told me, "I'm serious, Dad. Can you help?" I put my best hamster-healer look on my face and followed him into his bedroom.

One of the little rodents was indeed lying on his back, looking stressed. I immediately knew what to do. (Call my wife.) "Honey," I called, "come look at the hamster!" "Oh, my gosh," my wife diagnosed after a minute. "She's having babies." "What?" My son demanded. "But their names are Bert and Ernie, Mom!"

I was equally outraged. "Hey, how can that be? I thought we said we didn't want them to reproduce!" I accused my wife. Well, what do you want me to do, post a sign in their cage?!"She inquired. (I actually think she had the gull to say this sarcastically.) No, but you were supposed to get two boys!" I reminded her (in my most loving, calm, sweet voice, while gritting my teeth together). Yeah, Bert & Ernie!" My son agreed. "Well, it's just a little hard to tell on some guys, ya know," she informed me. (Again with the sarcasm,) ya think?)

By now the rest of the family had gathered to see what was going on. I shrugged, deciding to make the best of it. "Kids, this is going to be a wondrous experience," I announced. "We're about to witness the miracle of birth." "OH, Gross!" They shrieked. "Well, isn't THAT just great! What are we going to do with a litter of tiny little hamster babies?" My wife wanted to know. (I really do think she was being snotty here, too) Don't you?)

We peered at the patient. After much struggling, what looked like a tiny foot would appear briefly, vanishing a scant second later. "We don't appear to be making much progress," I noted. "It's a breech," my wife whispered, horrified. "Do something, Dad!" My son urged. "Okay, okay." Squeamishly, I reached in and grabbed the foot when it next appeared, giving it a gingerly tug. It disappeared. I tried several more times with the same results. "Should I call 911?" My eldest daughter wanted to know," Maybe they could talk us through the trauma." (You see a pattern here with the females in my house?)

"Let's get Ernie to the vet," I said grimly. We drove to the vet with my son holding the cage in his lap. "Breathe, Ernie, breathe," he urged. "I don't think hamsters do Lamaze," his mother noted to him. (Women can be so cruel to their own young. I mean what she does to ME is one thing, but this boy is of her womb.)

The vet took Ernie back to the examining room and peered at the little animal through a magnifying glass. "What do you think, Doc, a c-section?" I suggested scientifically. My son appeared impressed by my observation. "Oh, very interesting," he murmured. "Mr. and Mrs. Cameron, may I speak to you privately for a moment?" I gulped, nodding for my son to step outside. "Is Ernie going to be okay?" my wife asked. "Oh, perfectly," the vet assured us. "This hamster is not in labor. In fact, that isn't EVER going to happen....... Ernie is a boy." "What?" "You see, Ernie is a young male AND occasionally, as they come into maturity, like most male species, they um .... er ... masturbate, just the way he did, lying on his back." He blushed, glancing at my wife. "Well, you know what I'm saying Mr. Cameron!"

We were silent, absorbing this. "So Ernie's just ... just ... excited?"! My wife offered. "Exactly," the vet replied, relieved that we understood. More silence. Then my vicious, cruel wife started to giggle. And laugh. And then even laugh loudly! What's so funny?" I demanded, knowing, but not believing that the woman I married would commit the upcoming affront to my flawless manliness.

Tears were now running down her face. "It's just that I'm picturing you pulling on its ... its ... teeny little ..." she gasped for more air to bellow in laughter once more. "That's enough," I warned. We thanked the Veterinarian and hurriedly bundled the hamsters and our son back into the car. He was glad everything was going to be okay. "I know Ernie's really thankful for what you've done, Dad," he told me. "Oh, you have NO idea," my wife agreed, once again collapsing into laughter. Enough said.

THE NEXT TIME YOU THINK YOU ARE HAVING A BAD DAY

Fire authorities in California found a corpse in a burned out section of forest while assessing the damage done by a forest fire. The deceased male was dressed in a full wet suit, complete with scuba tanks on his back, flippers, and facemask. A post-mortem revealed that the person died not from burns but from massive internal injuries. Dental records provided a positive identification.

Investigators then set about to determine how a fully clad diver ended up in the middle of a forest fire. It was revealed that on the day of the fire, the person went for a diving trip off the coast some 20 miles from the forest. The fire fighters, seeking to control the fire as quickly as possible, called in a fleet of helicopters with very large dip buckets. Water was dipped from the ocean and then flown to the forest fire and emptied. You guessed it. One minute our diver was making like Flipper in the Pacific, the next he was doing the breaststroke in a fire dip bucket 300 feet in the air. Apparently he extinguished exactly 5'10" of the fire.

Some days it just doesn't pay to get out of bed. This article was taken from the California Examiner, March 20, 1998

STILL THINK YOU ARE HAVING A BAD DAY?

A man was working on his motorcycle on his patio and his wife was in the kitchen. The man was racing the engine on the motorcycle when it accidentally slipped into gear. The man, still holding onto the handle bars, was dragged through the glass patio doors and along with the motorcycle dumped onto the floor inside the house.

The wife, hearing the crash, ran into the dining room and found her husband lying on the floor, cut and bleeding, the motorcycle lying next to him and the shattered patio door. The wife ran to the phone and summoned the ambulance because they lived on a fairly large hill, the wife went down the several flights of stairs to the street to escort the paramedics to her husband.

After the ambulance arrived and transported the man to the hospital, the wife up righted the motorcycle and pushed it outside. Seeing that gas was spilled on the floor, the wife got some paper towels, blotted up the gasoline and threw the towels in the toilet. The man was treated and released to come home.

Upon arriving home, he looked at the shattered patio door and the damage done to his motorcycle. He became despondent, went to the bathroom, sat down on the toilet and smoked a cigarette. After finishing the cigarette, he flipped it between his legs into the toilet bowl while seated. The wife, who was in the kitchen, heard the loud explosion and her husband screaming.

She ran into the bathroom and found her husband lying on the floor. His trousers had been blown away and he was suffering burns on the buttocks, the back of his legs, and his groin.

The wife again ran to the phone to call the ambulance. The very same paramedic crew was dispatched and the wife met them at the street. The paramedics loaded the husband on to the stretcher and began carrying him to the street. While they were going down the stairs to the street accompanied by the wife, one of the paramedics asked the wife how the husband had burned himself.

She told them and the paramedics started laughing so hard, one of them slipped and tipped the stretcher, dumping the husband out. He fell down the remaining stairs and broke his arm. (Taken from a Florida Newspaper.)

Next time you think you're having a bad day recall: Received off the internet, no authorship given.

Iraqi terrorist, Khay Rahnajet, didn't pay enough postage on a letter bomb. It came back with "Return to Sender" stamped on it. Forgetting it was the bomb, he opened it and was blown to bits.

Purported to be true:

The average cost of rehabilitating a seal after the Exxon Valdez oil spill in Alaska was $80,000. At a special ceremony, two of the most expensively saved animals were released back into the wild amid cheers and applause from onlookers. A minute later they were both eaten by a killer whale.

A psychology student in New York rented out her spare room to a carpenter in order to nag him constantly and study his reactions. After weeks of needling, he snapped and proceeded to beat her repeatedly with an ax leaving her mentally retarded.

A woman came home to find her husband in the kitchen, shaking frantically with what looked like a wire running from his waist towards the electric kettle. Intending to jolt him away from the deadly current she whacked him with a handy plank of wood by the back door, breaking his arm in two places. Till that moment he had been happily listening to his Walkman.

Purported to be a true story;

Two animal rights protesters were protesting at the cruelty of sending pigs to a slaughterhouse in Bonn. Suddenly the pigs, all two-thousand of them, escaped through a broken fence and stampeded, trampling the two hapless protesters to death.

A FARMER'S STORY...(Lewis Grizzard told this so well)

A farmer had five female pigs and, as times were hard, he had determined to take them to the county fair and sell them. While at the fair, he met another farmer who owned five male pigs. After talking a bit, they decided to mate the pigs and split everything 50/50. The farmers lived sixty miles away from each other and so they each agreed to drive thirty miles and find a field midway in which to mate their pigs.

The first morning, the farmer with the female pigs got up at 5am, loaded the pigs into the family station wagon, which was the only vehicle they had, and drove the thirty miles. While the pigs were mating, he asked the other farmer, "How will I know if they are pregnant?" The other farmer replied, "If they're in the grass grazing in the morning, then they're pregnant, if they're in the mud, then they're not."

The next morning they were rolling in the mud, so he hosed them off, loaded them again into the family station wagon and proceeded to try again. The following morning, MUD again !!

This continued all week until one morning the farmer was so tired that he couldn't get out of bed. He called to his wife, "Honey, please look outside and tell me if the pigs are in the mud or in the field."
"Neither," yelled his wife, "they're in the station wagon and one of them is honking the horn.

CAT GOT YOUR TONGUE?
Calling in sick to work makes me uncomfortable. No matter how legitimate my illness, I always sense my boss thinks I am lying. On one occasion, I had a valid reason, but lied anyway because the truth was too humiliating. I simply mentioned that I had sustained a head injury and I hoped I would feel up to coming in the next day. By then, I could think up a dozy to explain the bandage on my crown.

The accident occurred mainly because I conceded to my wife's wishes to adopt a cute little kitty. Initially the new acquisition was no problem, but one morning I was taking my shower after breakfast when I heard my wife, Deb, call out to me from the kitchen. "Ed, the garbage disposal is dead. Come reset it." You know where the button is." I protested through the shower (pitter-patter). "Reset it yourself!"

"I am scared!" She pleaded. "What if it starts going and sucks me in?" (Pause) "C'mon, it'll only take a second." So out I came, dripping wet and butt naked, hoping to make a statement about how her cowardly behavior was not without consequence. I crouched down and stuck my head under the sink to find the button. It is the last action I remember performing. It struck without warning, without respect to my circumstances.

Nay, it wasn't a hexed disposal drawing me into its gnashing metal teeth. It was our new kitty, clawing playfully at the dangling objects she spied between my legs. She had been poised around the corner and stalked me as I took the bait under the sink. At precisely the second I was most vulnerable, she leapt at the toys I unwittingly offered and snagged them with her needle-like claws.

Now when men feel pain or even sense danger anywhere close to their masculine region, they lose all rational thought to control orderly bodily movements. Instinctively, their nerves compel the body to contort inwardly, while rising upwardly at a violent rate of speed of which even a well-trained monk could calmly stand, with his groin supporting the full weight of a kitten and rectify the situation in a step-by-step manner.

Wild animals are sometimes faced with a "fight or flight" syndrome. Men, in this predicament, choose only the "flight" option. Fleeing straight up, I knew at that moment how a cat feels when it is alarmed. It was a dismal irony. But, whereas cats seek great heights to escape, I never made it that far. The sink and cabinet bluntly impeded my ascent; the impact knocked me out cold.

When I awoke, my wife and the paramedics stood over me. Having been fully briefed by my wife, the paramedics snorted as they tried to conduct their work while suppressing their hysterical laughter.

At the office, colleagues tried to coax an explanation out of me but I kept silent, claiming it was too painful to talk. "What's the matter, cat got your tongue?" Boy, if they had only known. . .

Top 10 Ways to Tell When You have Joined a Cheap HMO:

10. Annual breast exam conducted at Hooters.

9. Directions to your doctor's office include, "take a left when you enter the trailer park."

8. Tongue depressors taste faintly of Fudgesicle.

7. Only proctologist in the plan is "Gus" from Roto-Rooter.

6. Only item listed under Preventive Care coverage is "an apple a day".

5. Your "primary care physician" is wearing the pants you gave to Goodwill

4. "Patient responsible for 200% of out-of-network charges" is not a typo.

3. The only expense covered 100% is embalming.

2. With your last HMO, your Prozac didn't come in different colors with little "M"s on them.

And Number 1 Sign You've Joined a Cheap HMO...
1. You ask for Viagra. You get a Popsicle stick and duct tape.

Top 10 Ways To Torment A Telemarketer: Received via email, No Authorship Given

10. When they ask "How are you today?" Tell them! "I'm so glad you asked because no one these days seems to care, and I have all these problems; my arthritis is acting up, my eyelashes are sore, my dog just died...."

9. If they say they're John doe from XYZ Company, ask them to spell their name. Then ask them to spell the company name. Then ask them where it is located. Continue asking them personal questions or questions about their company for as long as necessary.

8. Cry out in surprise, "Judy! Is that you? Oh my gosh! Judy, how have you been?" Hopefully, this will give Judy a few brief moments of pause as she tries to figure out where the hell she could know you from.

7. If MCI calls trying to get you to sign up for the Family and Friends Plan, reply, in as SINISTER a voice as you can, "I don't have any friends.... Would you be my friend?"

6. If they want to loan you money, tell them you just filed for bankruptcy and you could sure use some of it.

5. Tell the telemarketer you are on "home incarceration" and ask if they could bring you a case of beer and some chips.

4. After the telemarketer gives their spiel, ask him/her to marry you. When they get all flustered, tell them that you could not just give your credit card number to a complete stranger.

3. Tell the telemarketer you are busy at the moment and ask them if they will give you their HOME phone number so you can call them back. When the telemarketer explains that they cannot give out their HOME number, you say "I guess you don't want anyone bothering you at home, right?" The telemarketer will agree, and you say, "Now you know how I feel! Say good-bye and hang up.

2. Insist that the caller is really your buddy Leon, playing a joke. Come on Leon, cut it out! Seriously, Leon, how's your momma?"

And number One:
1. Tell them to talk VERY SLOWLY because you want to write EVERY WORD down.

Forwarded message: Received on the Internet: No Authorship Given
The story behind the letter below is that there is this nut case in Newport, VT named Scott Williams who digs things out of his back yard and sends the stuff he finds to the Smithsonian Institute, labeling them with scientific names, insisting that they are actual archaeological finds. This guy really exists and does this in his spare time! Anyway... here's the actual response from the Smithsonian Institution.

Bear this in mind next time you think you are challenged in your duty to respond to a difficult situation in writing.

Smithsonian Institute
207 Pennsylvania Avenue
Washington, DC 20078

Dear Mr. Williams,

Thank you for your latest submission to the Institute, labeled 93211-D, layer seven, next to the clothesline post...Hominid skull."

We have given this specimen a careful and detailed examination, and regret to inform you that we disagree with your theory that it represents conclusive proof of the presence of Early Man in Charleston County two million years ago.

Rather, it appears that what you have found is the head of a Barbie doll, of the variety that one of our staff, who has small children, believes to be "Malibu Barbie."

It is evident that you have given a great deal of thought to the analysis of this specimen, and you may be quite certain that those of us who are familiar with your prior work in the field were loath to come to contradiction with your findings. However, we do feel that there are a number of physical attributes of the specimen, which might have tipped you off to its modern origin:

1. The material is molded plastic. Ancient hominid remains are typically fossilized bone.

2. The cranial capacity of the specimen is approximately 9 cubic centimeters, well below the threshold of even the earliest identified proto-hominids.

3. The dentition pattern evident on the skull is more consistent with the common domesticated dog than it is with the ravenous man-eating Pliocene clams you speculate roamed the wetlands during that time.

This latter finding is certainly one of the most intriguing hypotheses you have submitted in your history with this institution, but the evidence seems to weigh rather heavily against it. Without going into too much detail, let us say that:

A. *The specimen looks like the head of a Barbie doll that a dog has chewed on.*

B. *Clams don't have teeth.*

It is with feelings tinged with melancholy that we must deny your request to have the specimen carbon-dated. This is partially due to the heavy load our lab must bear in its normal operation, and partly due to carbon-dating to be notorious for inaccuracy in fossils of recent geologic record. To the best of our knowledge, no Barbie dolls were produced prior to 1956 AD, and carbon-dating is likely to produce wildly inaccurate results.

Sadly, we must also deny your request that we approach the National Science Foundation Phylogeny Department with the concept of assigning your specimen the scientific name Australopithecus Spiff-Arino. Speaking personally, I for one, fought tenaciously for the acceptance of your proposed taxonomy, but was ultimately voted down because the species name you selected was hyphenated, and didn't really sound like it might be Latin.

However, we gladly accept your generous donation of this fascinating specimen to the museum. While it is undoubtedly not a Hominid fossil, it is nonetheless yet another riveting example of the great body of work you seem to accumulate here so effortlessly. You should know that our Director has reserved a special shelf in his own office for the display of the specimens you have previously submitted to the Institution, and the entire staff speculates daily on what you will happen upon next in your digs at the site you have discovered in your Newport back yard.

We eagerly anticipate your trip to our nation's capital that you proposed in your last letter, and several of us are pressing the Director to pay for it. We are particularly interested in hearing you expand on your theories surrounding the trans-positating fillifitation of ferrous ions in a structural matrix that makes the excellent juvenile Tyrannosaurus rex femur you recently discovered take on the deceptive appearance of a rusty 9-mm Sears Craftsman automotive crescent wrench.

Yours in Science,

ARCHAEOLOGISTS:

A team of archaeologists was excavating in Israel when they came upon a cave. Written across the wall of the cave were the following symbols, in this order of appearance: A woman, a donkey, a shovel, a fish, and a Star of David.

It was considered a unique find and the writings were said to be at least three thousand years old. The piece of stone was removed, brought to the museum, and archaeologists from around the world came to study the ancient symbols. They held a huge meeting after months of conferences to discuss the meaning of the markings. The President of the society pointed at the first drawing and said "This looks like a woman. We can judge that this race was family oriented and held women in high esteem. You can also tell they were intelligent, as the next symbol resembles a donkey, so they were smart enough to have animals help them till the soil. The next drawing looks like a shovel of some sort, which means they even had tools to help them. Even further proof of their high intelligence is the fish which means that if a famine had hit the earth, whereby the food didn't grow, they would take to the sea for food.

The last symbol appears to be the Star of David which means they were evidently Hebrews." The audience applauded enthusiastically. But, a little old man stood up in the back of the room and said, "Idiots! Hebrew is read from right to left. It says: 'Holy Mackerel, Dig The Ass On That Woman!'"

Harvey Rowe

Chief Curator- Antiquities

Received via email, no authorship given:

The Following has been rumored as a supposed letter a person wrote a letter to the White House complaining about the treatment of a captive taken during the Afghanistan war. Attached is a copy of a letter they received back:

White House
1600 Pennsylvania Avenue
Washington, D.C.20001

Dear Concerned Citizen:

Thank you for your recent letter roundly criticizing our treatment of the Taliban and Al Qaeda detainees currently being held at Guantanamo Bay, Cuba. My administration takes these matters seriously, and your opinion was heard loud and clear, here in Washington.

You'll be pleased to learn that, thanks to the concerns of citizens like you, we are creating a new division of the Terrorist Retraining Program, to be called the "Liberals accept Responsibility for Killers" program, or LARK for short.

In accordance with the guidelines of this new program, we have decided to place one terrorist under your personal care. Your personal detainee has been selected and scheduled for transportation under heavily armed guard to your residence next Monday. Ali Mohammed Ahmed bin Mahmud (you can just call him Ahmed) is to be cared for pursuant to the standards you personally demanded in your letter of admonishment.

It will likely be necessary for you to hire some assistant caretakers. We will conduct weekly inspections to ensure that your standards of care for Ahmed are commensurate with those you so strongly recommended in your letter.

Ahmed's meal requirements are simple, but we strongly suggest serving meals that do not require utensils, particularly knives and forks. Also, these should be "one-handed" foods; Ahmed will not eat with his left hand since he uses it to wipe himself after purging his bowels (which he will do in your yard) - but look on the bright side, there will be no increase in the toilet paper bill.

He generally bathes quarterly with the change of seasons, assuming that it rains, and he washes his clothes simultaneously. This should help with your water bill. Also, your new friend has a really bad case of body lice that hasn't been completely remedied.

Please heed the large orange notice attached to your detainee's cage: "Does not play well with others. Although Ahmed is sociopathic and extremely violent, we hope that your sensitivity to what you described as his "attitudinal problem" will help him overcome these character flaws. Perhaps you are correct in describing these problems as mere cultural differences.

He will bite you, given the chance, but his rabies test came back negative so not to worry. We understand that you plan to offer counseling and home schooling. Your adopted terrorist is extremely proficient in hand-to-hand combat and can extinguish human life with such simple items as a pencil or nail clippers. We do not suggest that you ask him to demonstrate these skills at your next yoga group.

He is also expert at making a wide variety of explosive devices from common household products, so you may wish to keep those items locked up, unless (in your opinion) this might offend him.

Ahmed will not wish to interact with your wife or daughters (except sexually) since he views females as a subhuman form of property. However, he will be eager to assist with the education of your sons; have available for their use several copies of the Quran.

Oh - and rest assured he absolutely loves animals, especially cats and dogs. He prefers them roasted, but raw is fine, too, if they aren't more than 2 or 3 days dead.

Thanks again for your letter. We truly appreciate it when folks like you, who know so much, keep us informed of the proper way to do our job. We think this watching over each other's shoulder is such a good way for people to interact that we will be sending a team of federal officials with expertise in your line of work to your place of business soon, just to help you do your job better.

Don't be concerned that they have the power to close your business, seize your property, and arrest you for any violation of the 4,850,206 laws, codes, regulations and rules that apply to your profession. They're really there just to make sure you're doing everything the proper way. That is what you wanted, right?

Well, thank you for this opportunity to interact with such a valued member of the citizenry. You take good care of Ahmed – and remember... we'll be watching.

Cordially,
Your Buddy,
Dubbya

This one is a genuine hoot. It was an actual letter sent to a man named Ryan DeVries by the Michigan Department of Environmental Quality, State of Michigan. Wait till you read this guy's response...
Received via email, no authorship given:

Mr. Ryan DeVries 2088 Dagget Pierson, MI 49339
SUBJECT: DEQ File No. 97-59-0023; T11N; R10W, Sec. 20; Montcalm County

Dear Mr. DeVries:

It has come to the attention of the Department of Environmental Quality that there has been recent unauthorized activity on the above referenced parcel of property. You have been certified as the legal landowner and/or contractor who did the following unauthorized activity: Construction and maintenance of two wood debris dams across the outlet stream of Spring Pond.

A permit must be issued prior to the start of this type of activity. A review of the Department's files shows that no permits have been issued. Therefore, the Department has determined that this activity is in violation of Part 301, Inland Lakes and Streams, of the Natural Resource and Environmental Protection Act, Act 451 of the Public Acts of 1994, being sections 324.30101 to 324.30113 of the Michigan Compiled Laws, annotated.

The Department has been informed that one or both of the dams partially failed during a recent rain event, causing debris and flooding at downstream locations. We find that dams of this nature are inherently hazardous and cannot be permitted. The Department therefore orders you to cease and desist all activities at this location, and to restore the stream to a free-flow condition by removing all wood and brush forming the dams from the stream channel. All restoration work shall be completed no later than January 31, 2002.

Please notify this office when the restoration has been completed so that a follow-up site inspection may be scheduled by our staff. Failure to comply with this request or any further unauthorized activity on the site may result in this case being referred for elevated enforcement action.

We anticipate and would appreciate your full cooperation in this matter. Please feel free to contact me at this office if you have any questions.

Sincerely,
David L. Price
District Representative Land and Water Management Division

This is the actual response sent back:

Dear Mr. Price,
Re: DEQ File No. 97-59-0023; T11N; R10W, Sec. 20; Montcalm County

Your certified letter dated 12/17/97 has been handed to me for response. First of all, Mr. Ryan DeVries is not the legal landowner and/or Contractor at 2088 Dagget, Pierson, Michigan. I am the legal owner and a couple of beavers are in the (State unauthorized) process of constructing and maintaining two wood "debris" dams across the outlet stream of my Spring Pond. While I did not pay for, authorize, nor supervise their dam project, I think they would be highly offended that you call their skillful use of nature's building materials "debris."

I would like to challenge your department to attempt to emulate their dam project any time and/or any place you choose. I believe I can safely state there is no way you could ever match their dam skills, their dam resourcefulness, their dam ingenuity, their dam persistence, their dam determination and/or their dam work ethic.

As to your request, I do not think the beavers are aware that they must first fill out a dam permit prior to the start of this type of dam activity. My first dam question to you is: (1) Are you trying to discriminate against my Spring Pond Beavers or (2) do you require all beavers throughout this state to conform to said dam request?

If you are not discriminating against these particular beavers, through the Freedom of Information Act, I request completed copies of all those other applicable beaver dam permits that have been issued. Perhaps we will see if there really is a dam violation of Part 301, Inland Lakes and Streams, of the Natural Resource and Environmental Protection Act, Act 451 of the Public Acts of 1994, being sections 324.30101 to 324.30113 of the Michigan Compiled Laws, annotated.

I have several concerns. My first concern is - aren't the beavers entitled to legal representation? The Spring Pond Beavers are financially destitute and are unable to pay for said representation so the State will have to provide them with a dam lawyer. The Department's dam concern that either one or both of the dams failed during a recent rain event causing flooding is proof that this is a natural occurrence, which the Department is required to protect. In other words, we should leave the Spring Pond Beavers alone rather than harassing them and calling their dam names.

If you want the stream "restored" to a dam free-flow condition please contact the beavers - but if you are going to arrest them, they obviously did not pay any attention to your dam letter they being unable to read English.

In my humble opinion, the Spring Pond Beavers have a right to build their unauthorized dams as long as the sky is blue, the grass is green and water flows downstream. They have more dam rights than I do to live and enjoy Spring Pond. If the Department of Natural Resources and Environmental Protection lives up to its name, it should protect the natural resources (beavers) and the environment (beavers' dams.).

So, as far as the beavers and I are concerned, this dam case can be referred for more elevated enforcement action right now. Why wait until 1/31/2002? The Spring Pond Beavers may be under the dam ice then and there will be no way for you or your dam staff to contact/harass them then.

In conclusion, I would like to bring to your attention to a real environmental quality (health) problem in the area. It is the bears! Bears are actually defecating in our woods. I definitely believe you should be persecuting the defecating bears and leave the beavers alone. If you are going to investigate the beaver dam, watch your step! (The bears are not careful where they dump!)

Being unable to comply with your dam request, and being unable to contact you on your dam answering machine, I am sending this response to your dam office.

Sincerely

"WHAT NOT TO CALL YOUR DOG"

EVERYBODY WHO HAS A DOG CALLS HIM "ROVER" OR "BOY." I CALL MINE "SEX"!

Now, Sex has been very embarrassing to me. When I went to City Hall to renew his Dog License, I told the clerk that I would like to have a license for Sex. He said, "I would like to have one too." Then I said, "But this is a dog." He said he didn't care what she looked like. Then I said, "You don't understand, I've had Sex since I was nine years old." He said that I must have been quite a kid!

When I got married and went on my honeymoon, I took the dog with me. I told the motel clerk that I wanted a room for Sex. He said that every room in the place was for Sex. I said, "You don't understand, Sex keeps me awake at night." The Clerk said, "Me too."

One day I entered Sex in a contest, but before the competition began, the dog ran away. Another contestant asked me why I was just standing there, looking around. I told him that I had planned to have Sex in the contest. He told me that I should have sold my own tickets. "But you don't understand," I said, "I had hoped to have Sex on TV." He called me a show-off.

When my wife and I separated, we went to court to fight for the custody of the dog. I said, "Your Honor, I had Sex before I was married." The judge said, "Me too," then I told him that after I was married, Sex left me. He said, "Me too."

Last night, Sex ran off again. I spent hours looking around town for him. A policeman came over to me and asked, "What are you doing in this alley at four o'clock in the morning?" I said, "I'm looking for Sex." My case comes up Friday.

Anonymous

"GASTRONOMICAL BEAN STORY"

Once upon a time there lived a man who had a maddening passion for baked beans. They always had a very embarrassing and somewhat lively reaction on him. Then one day he met a girl and fell in love. When it was apparent that they would marry, he thought to himself, "She is such a sweet and gentle girl, she will never go for this kind of carrying on." So he made the supreme sacrifice and gave up baked beans. They were married shortly thereafter.

Some months later, his car broke down on his way home from work, and since they lived in the country, he called his wife and told her that he would be late because he had to walk home. On his way he passed a small cafe and the odor of baked beans was overwhelming. Since he had several miles to walk he figured that he would work off any side effects before he got home and stopped at the cafe. Before leaving, he had eaten three large plates of baked beans. All the way home he putt-putted and after arriving he felt reasonably safe that he had putt-putted his last.

When he arrived at the house he noted his wife seemed somewhat agitated and excited to see him and explained delightedly, "Darling, I have the most wonderful surprise for dinner tonight." Then she blindfolded him and led him to his chair at the head of the table. He seated himself and just as she was ready to remove the blindfold, the telephone rang. She made him vow not to touch the blindfold until she had returned, then she went to answer the phone.

Seizing the opportunity, he shifted his weight to one leg and let go. It was not only loud but ripe as rotten eggs. He took his napkin from his lap and vigorously fanned the air about him. Things had just returned to normal when he felt another urge coming on. So, he shifted his weight to the other leg and let go again.

This was a truly a prize-winner. While keeping his ear on the conversation in the hall, he went on like this for ten minutes until he knew the phone farewell indicated the end of his freedom. He placed his napkin on his lap and folded his hands on top of it and smiling contentedly to himself. He was the picture of innocence when his wife returned and apologized for taking so long. She asked if he had peeked and he of course, assured her that he had not. At this point, she removed his blindfold, and there was his surprise............ Twelve dinner guests seated around the table for a Birthday Party for him.

THE ITALIAN WHO WENT TO DETROIT

One a day i go to-a to a bigga otel in Detroit andI go down to eata breakfast in de morning. I tella de waitress, "I wanna two piss's toast." She bringa me only one a piss. I tella her, "I wanna two piss." She tella me, 'Go to de toilet!'I say, "You no understand, I wanna two piss on my plate." She say, 'You better no piss on your plate you Sonna Ma Bitch!'I don't even know the lady and she call-a-me a Sonna Ma Bitch!

Later I go to Lunch ata bigga restaurant. The waitress bringa me a spoon anda knife but no fock. I tell her, "I wanna fock." She tella me, 'Everybody wanna fock but I don't get off till 5:30.'I tella her, "You no understand. I wanna fock on de table." She says, 'You better nota fock on de table you sonna-ma-bitch! 'So I go back to my room in de otel ana there's a-no sheet ona my bed. I call de manager and tella him, "I wanna sheet." He tella me da same ting, 'Go to de toilet.'I say, "You no understand--I wanna sheet on de bed." He tella me, 'You sheet ona de bed, we kicka your ass.'

De next morning I go to check outa de otel, ana de clerk behind de counter, he say, 'Peace to you.'I say, "Piss on you too, you sonna ma bitch--me go back to Italy."

The Train Ride

After returning from his honeymoon in Florida with his new bride Virginia. Luigi stopped in his New York neighborhood barbershop to say hello to his friends. Giovanni said, "Hey, Luigi. How was a da treep?" Luigi said, "Ever'thing was a perfect except for da train a ride down." "What'a you mean, Luigi?" asked Giovanni.

"Well, we boarda da train at Grand Centrala Station. My beautifula Virginia had packed a biga basket a food with vino and cigars for a me, and a we were looking a 'forward to da trip. All was OK until we gotta hungry and opened up a da luncha basket. The conductor came by, wagged his a finger at us and a say, 'No eat in dese'a car. Must'a use'a dining car.'"

"So, me and my beautiful'a Virginia, we go to dining car, eat a big'a lunch and begin to open'a bottle of vino! . Conductor walk by me again, wag his'a finger and say, 'No drink'a in dese'a car. Must'a use'a club'a car."

"So we go to club'a car. While'a drinking vino, I start to light'a my big'a cigar. The conductor, he wag'a his finger again and say, 'No smoke'a in dese'a car. Must'a go to smoker car.'"

"We go to smoker car and I smoke'a my cigar. Later, my beautiful Virginia and I, we go to sleeper car and'a go to bed. We just about to have'a sex and the conductor, he walk'a through car corridor shouting at top of his voice....

'NO-FOLK'A, VIRGINIA!' 'NO-FOLK'A VIRGINIA!"

Nexta time, Ima driva down to Florida"

Lightning Source UK Ltd.
Milton Keynes UK
UKHW041351060821
388423UK00001BA/81